The Big "H"

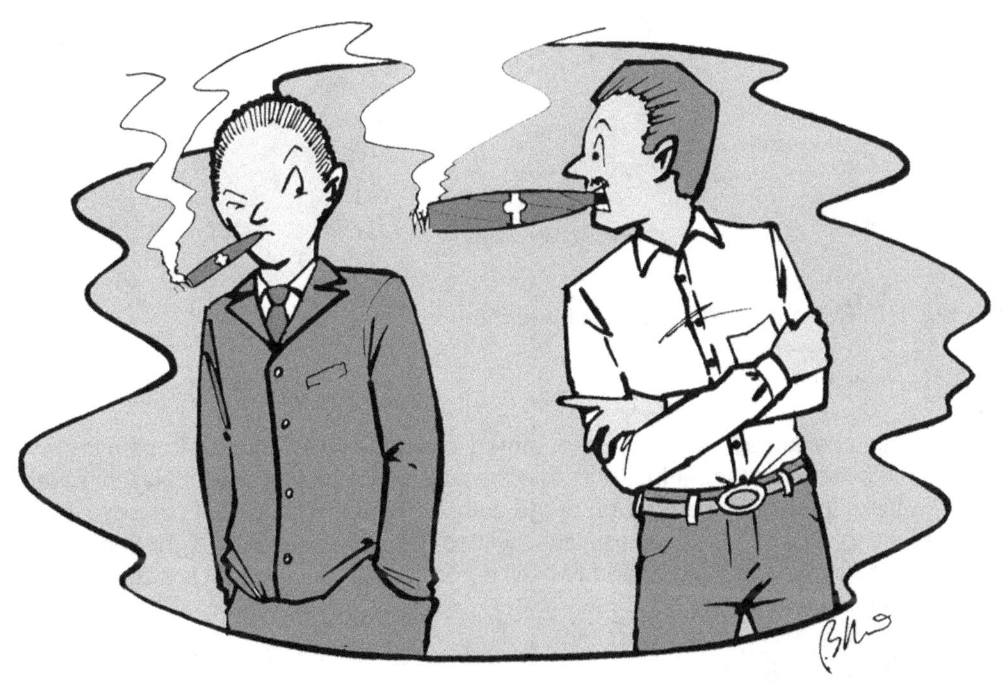

"Hey...looky here -- an ASSOCIATE PRODUCER!"

by B. Morino

This book is dedicated to everyone who's had to put up with my crap, my mood swings, my ill-placed humor, and my iPod beanie (a.k.a., the Musical Hat) which, from time to time, makes it seem like I couldn't care less of your existence, when in fact I simply can't hear a single word you're saying...

Which means, really, the hat is doing its job. Sorry, and thanks.

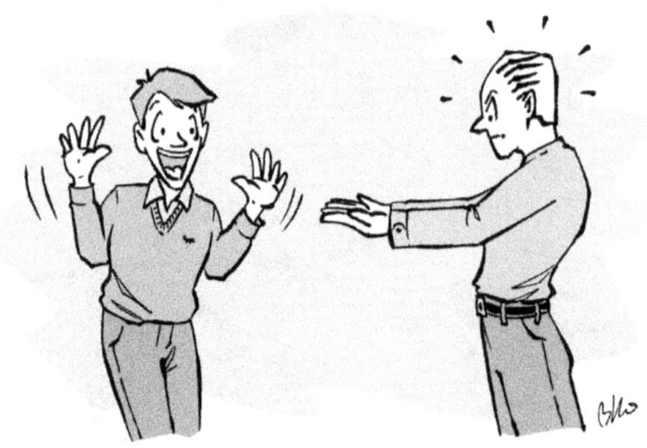

"Surprise!!! It's a VIRTUAL BUDGET!!!"

ISBN 0615564682
ISBN-13 978-0615564685

Written and illustrated by Brandon Morino Book and cover design by Brandon Morino

Published by

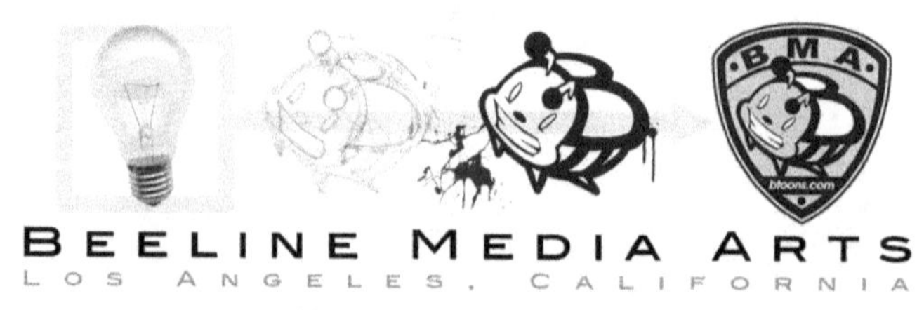

Table of Contents

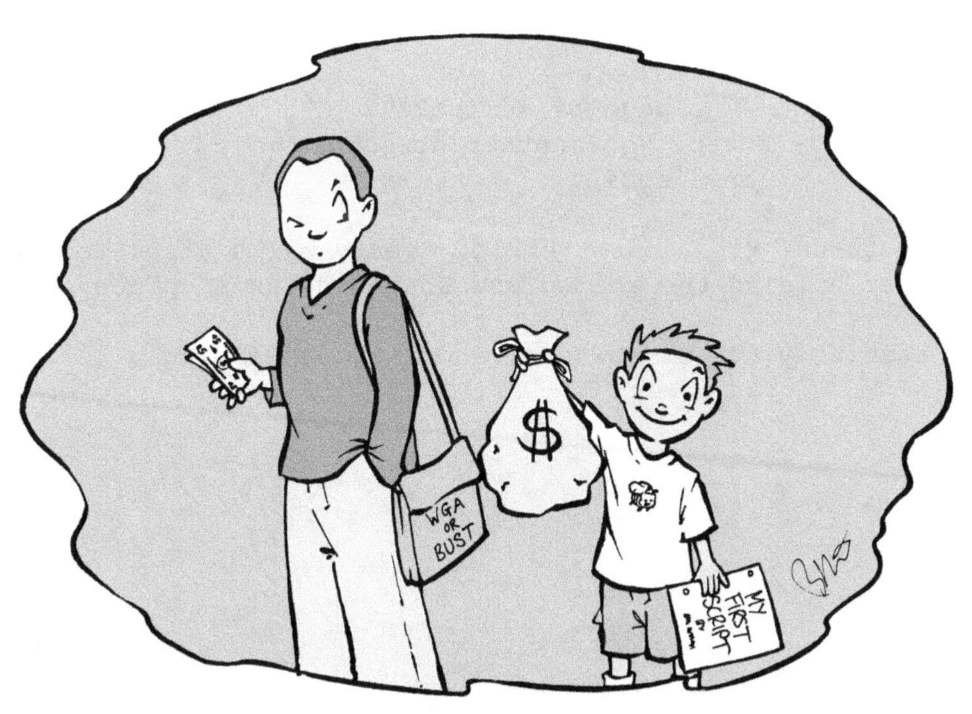

FADE IN

INT. CARTOON BOOK - DAY

The READER cracks open the cover of The Big H, with the anticipation of what lies inside. Across the copyright page, then past the table of contents. He emotes with a melodramatic --

READER
I blew a perfectly good power lunch to buy this garbage. It had better make me laugh.

His moment-before is that of a stray dog pissing on his left pantleg. The despondent reader needs some comic relief, and fast, or suffer a sense-memory of the same emotional breakdown he experienced five summers ago when his Traveling Shakespeare Festival played in Oakland. The unruly audience ran out of tomatoes, but found billiard balls the perfect substitute. Four thespians died that day, a day the reader shall never forget. He uses it to this day as his motivation.

READER
What is this --
(beat)
-- a page of script????
Crap. Not another screenplay in disguise.

The page turns. His hands tremble. Sweaty palms stick to the thin paper holding the shaped and shadowed ink in place.

Then, seemingly out of nowhere, and without warning...

1. OCCUPATIONAL HAZARDS

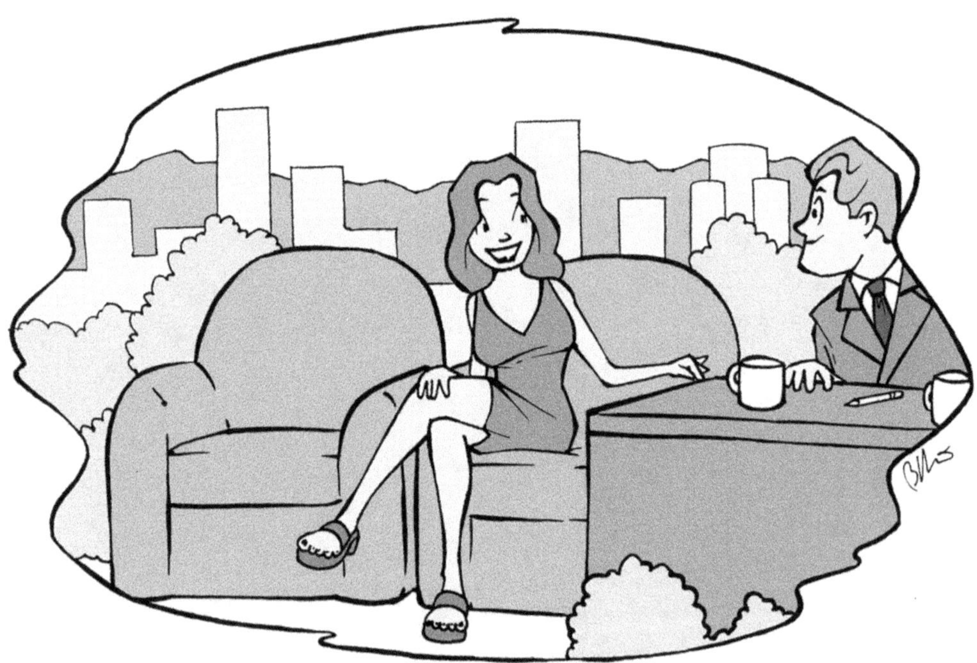

"The cancellation of my show released my deepest, darkest fears, Jay. Of worthlessness, of being unwanted. Only the power of my family brought me back from certain destruction....and a retreat to my private beach in Tahiti. That helped, too."

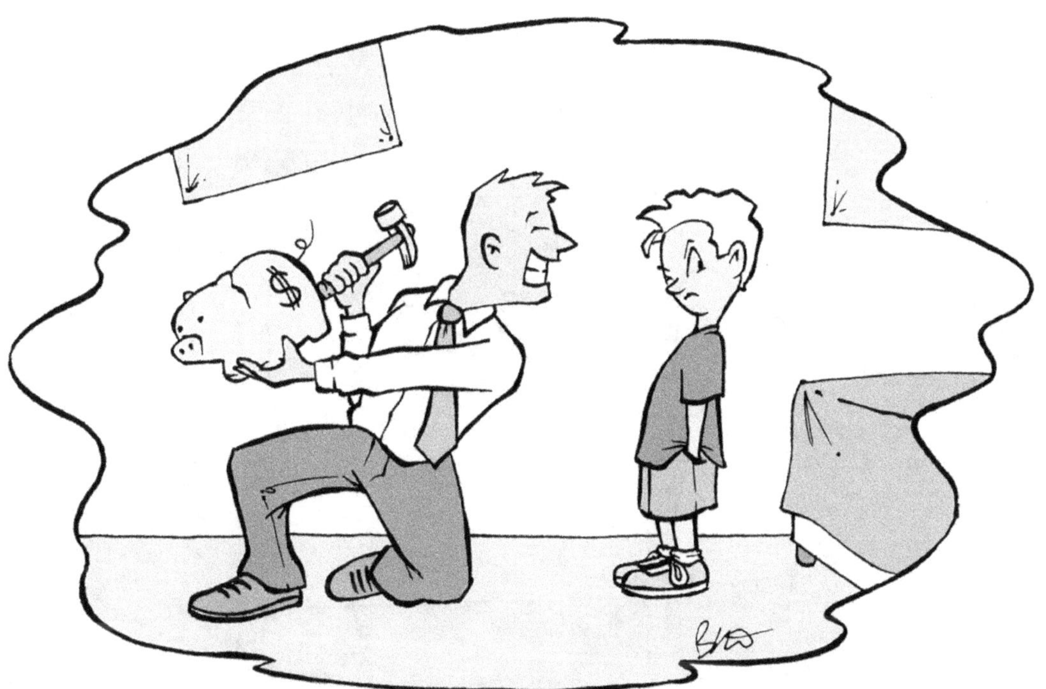

"I'm so PROUD of you, son....I'll give you associate producer credit, and .5% net points."

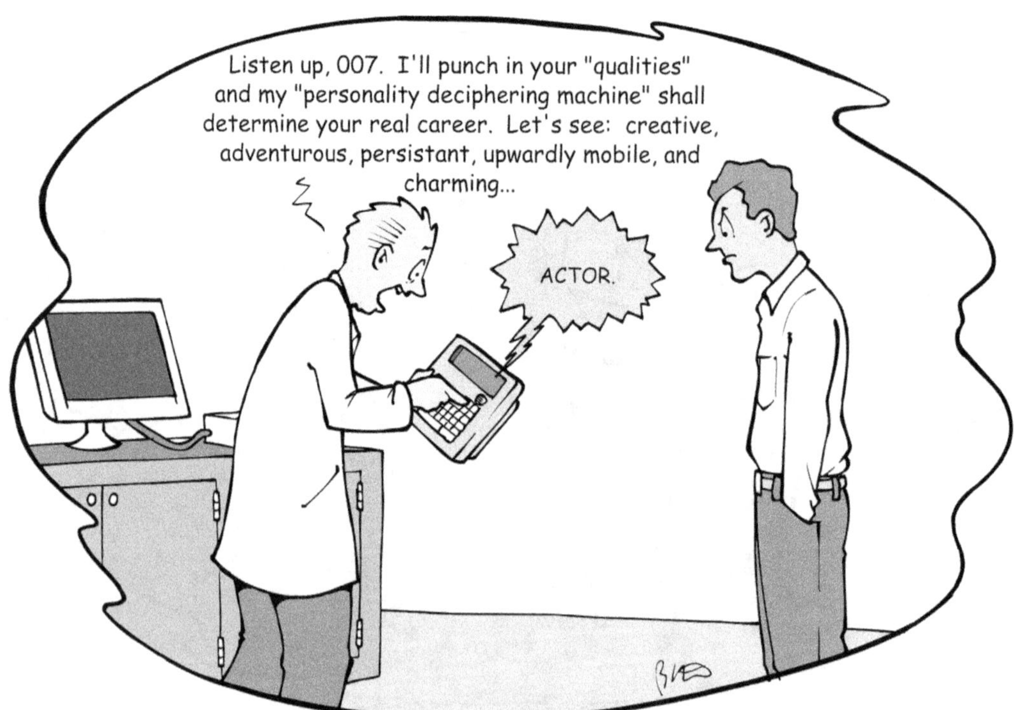

Q PISSES OFF JAMES BOND...FOR THE LAST TIME.

The Big "H"

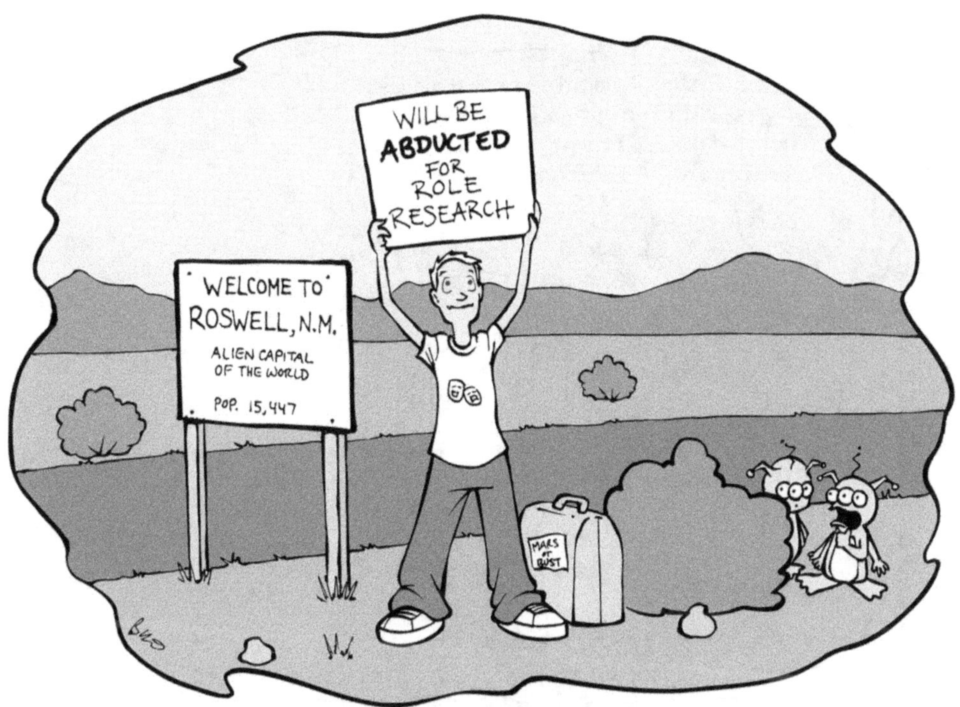

"I dunno, Ralph. I smell B-LIST."

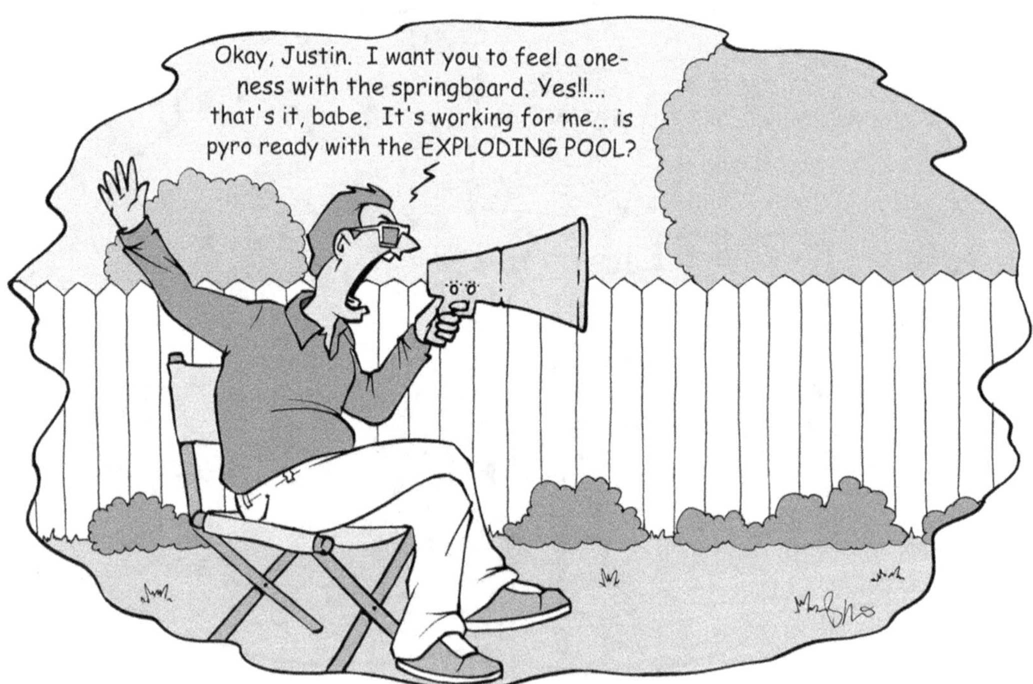

DIVING LESSONS...WITH MICHAEL BAY

The Big "H"

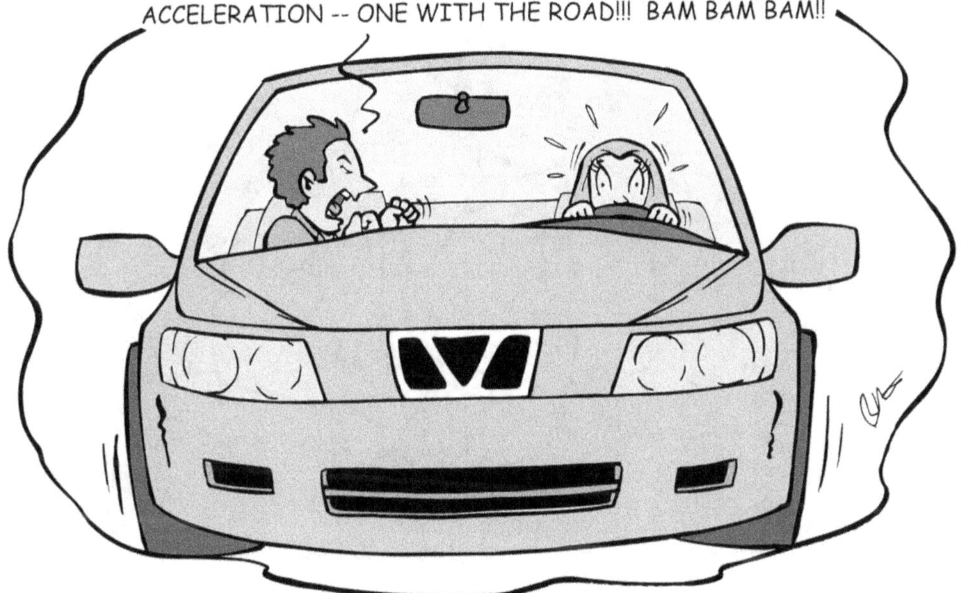

DRIVING LESSONS WITH AL PACINO

The Big "H"

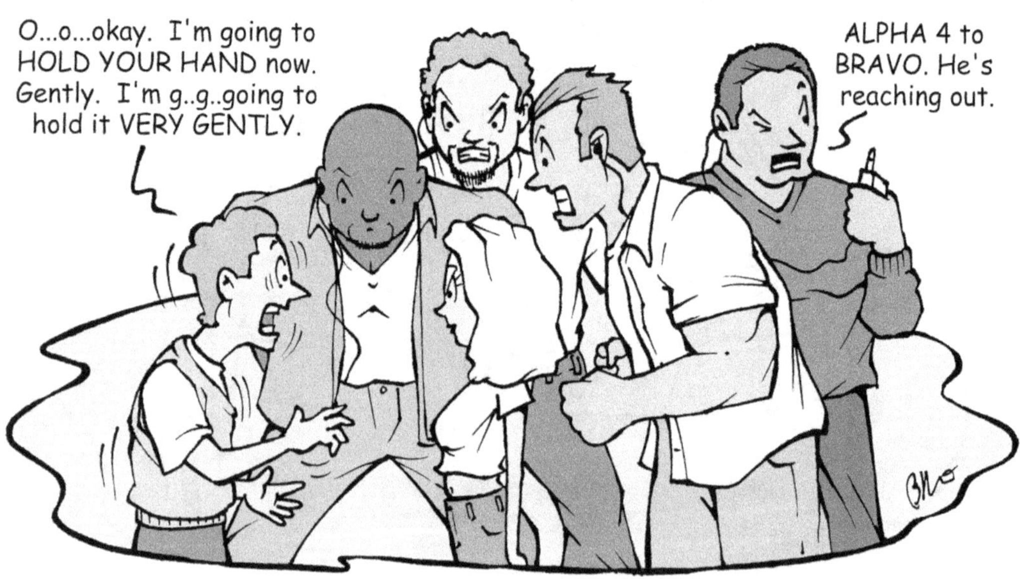
O...o...okay. I'm going to HOLD YOUR HAND now. Gently. I'm g..g..going to hold it VERY GENTLY.
ALPHA 4 to BRAVO. He's reaching out.

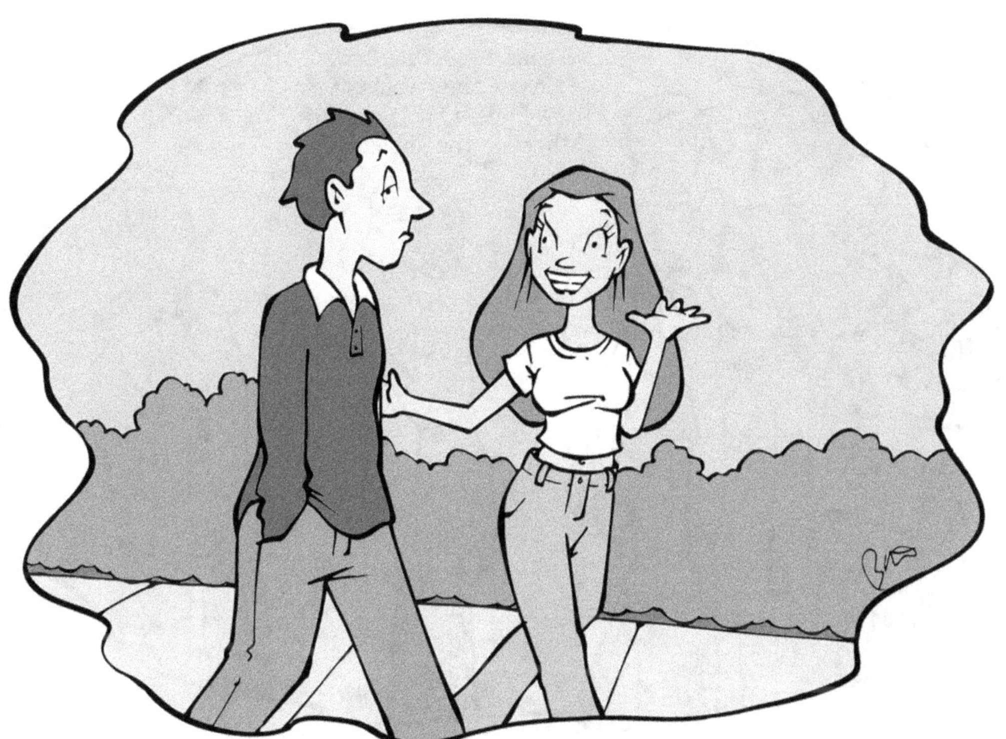

LET'S GO BY THE REFLECTING POOL AGAIN SO WE CAN SEE MYSELF.

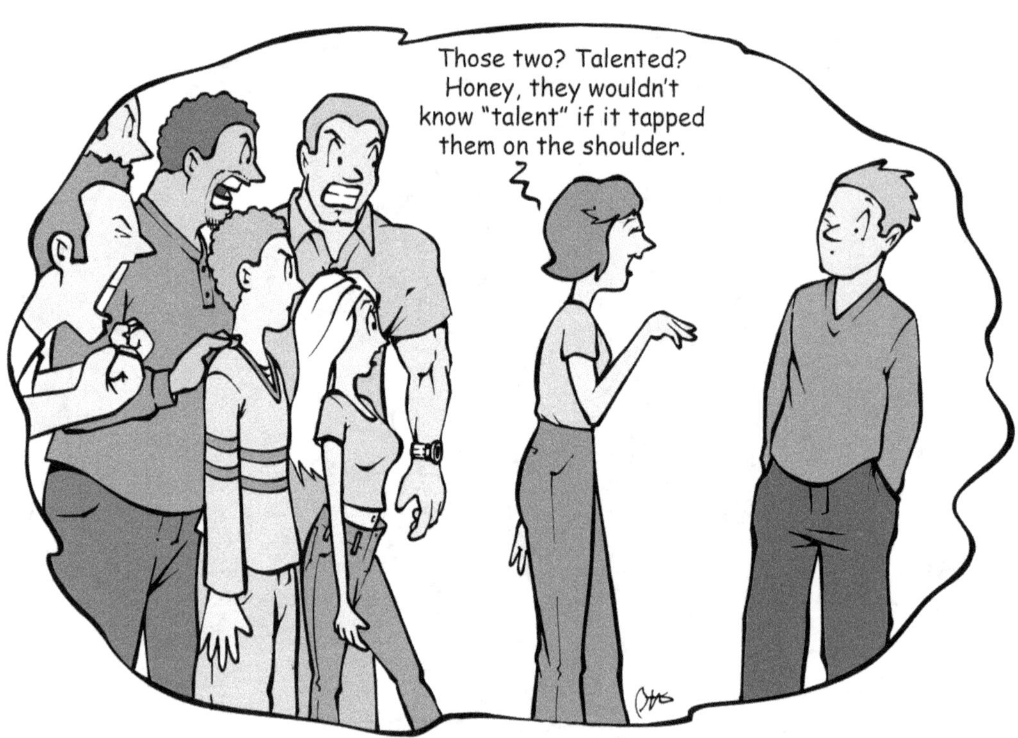

LOOK BOTH WAYS BEFORE TALKING

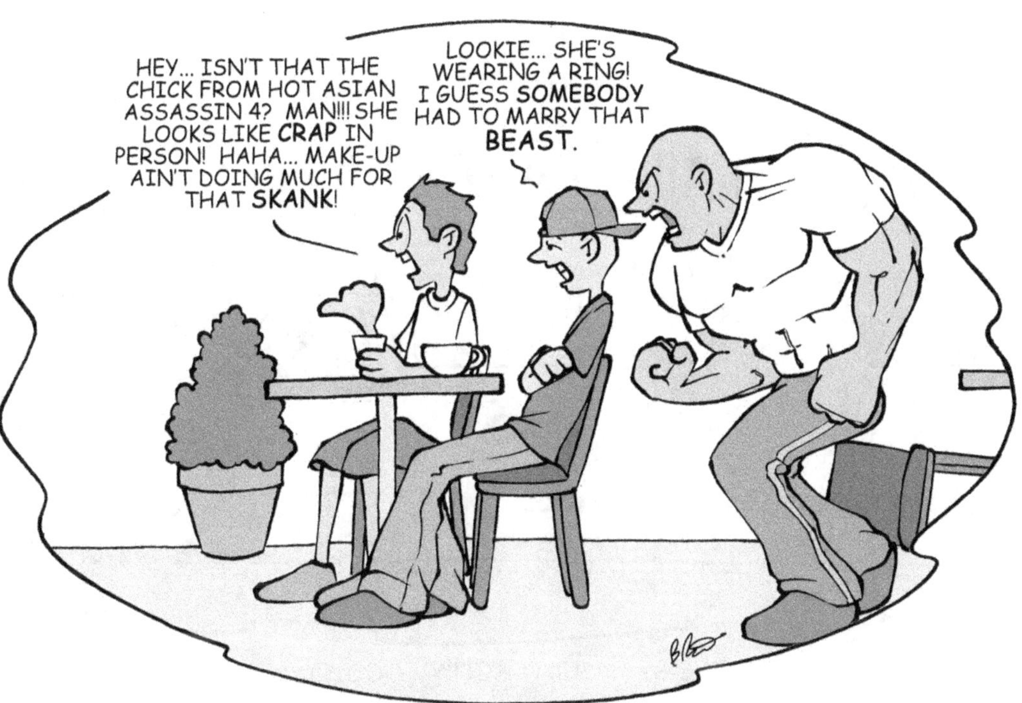

LOOK BOTH WAYS BEFORE TALKING

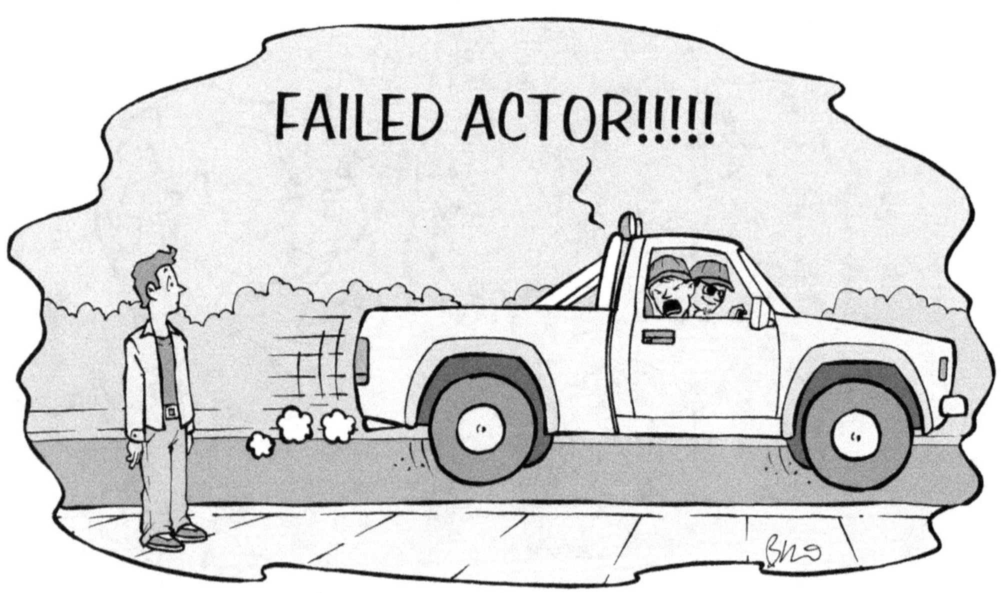

DRIVE-BY INSULT...HOLLYWOOD STYLE

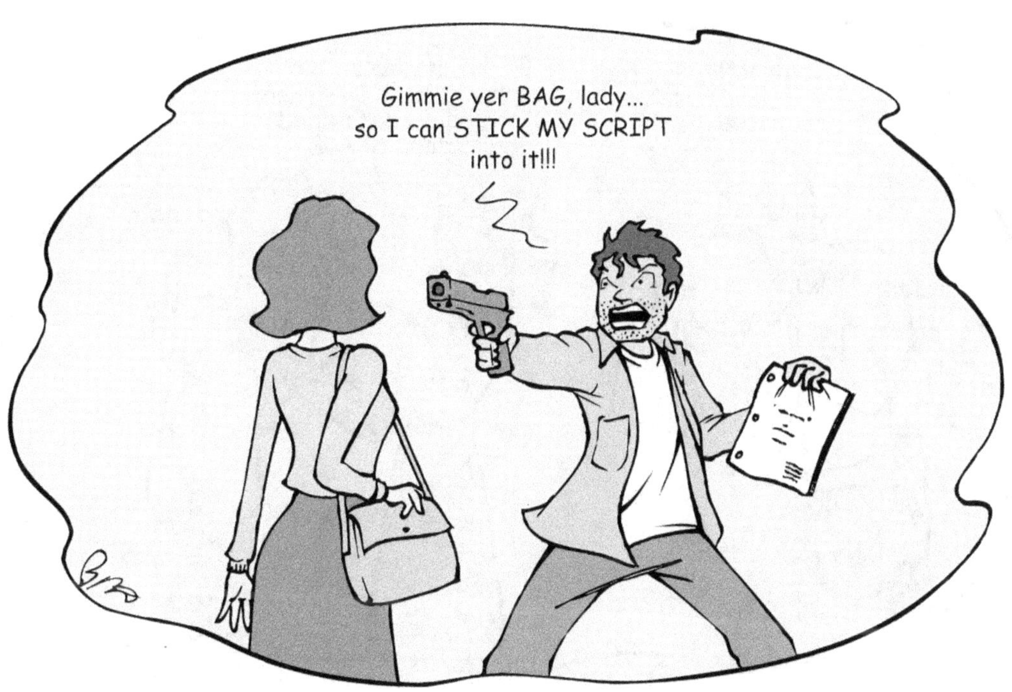
Gimmie yer BAG, lady...
so I can STICK MY SCRIPT
into it!!!

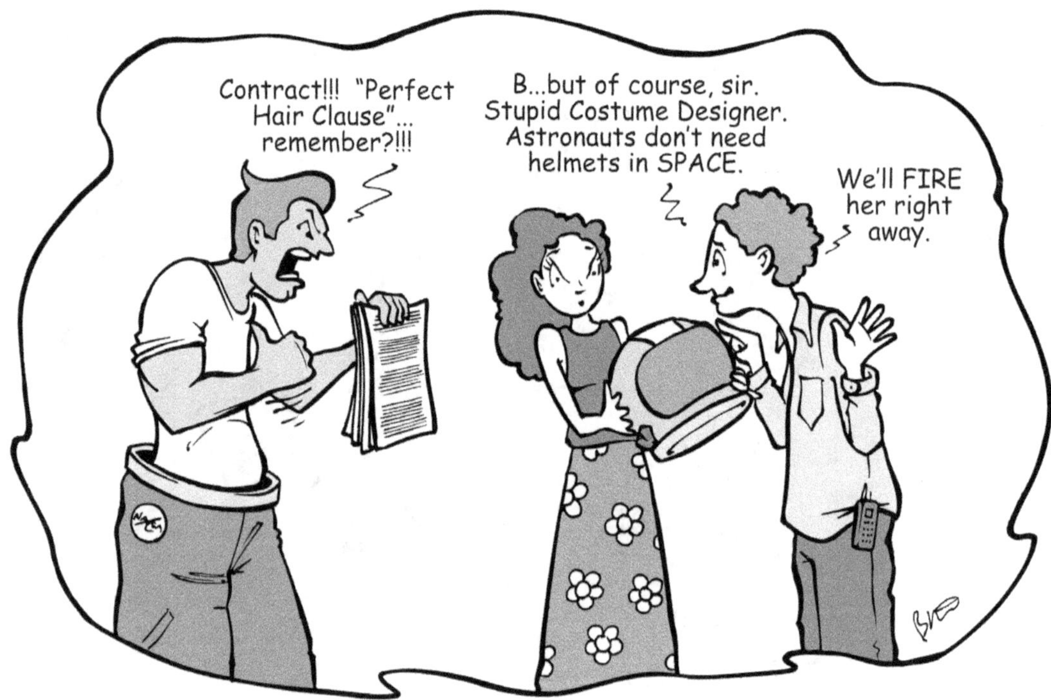
Contract!!! "Perfect Hair Clause"... remember?!!!
B...but of course, sir. Stupid Costume Designer. Astronauts don't need helmets in SPACE.
We'll FIRE her right away.

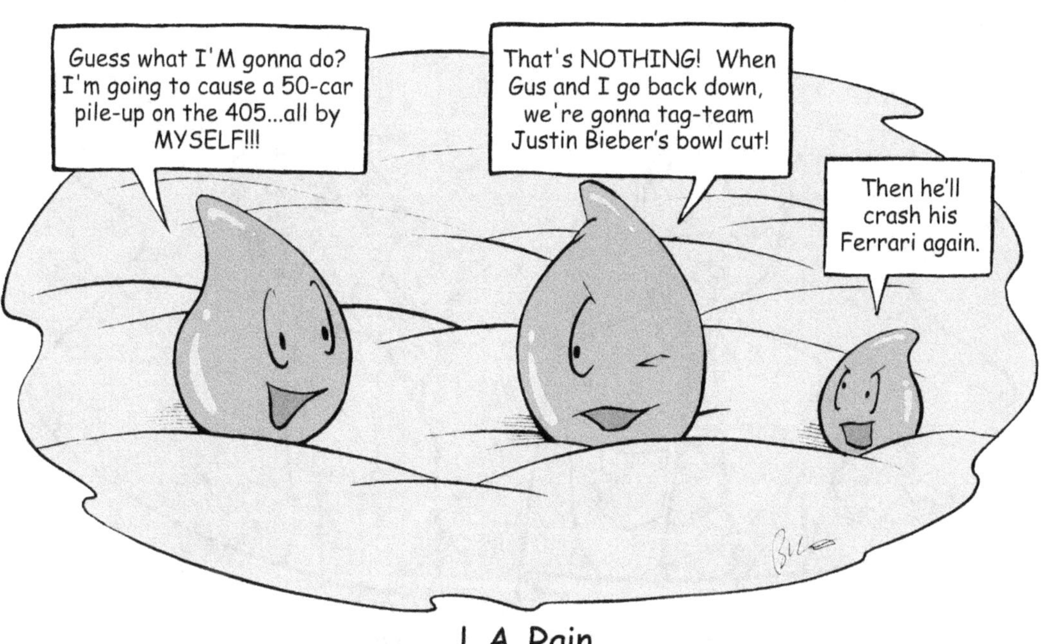
Guess what I'M gonna do? I'm going to cause a 50-car pile-up on the 405...all by MYSELF!!!
That's NOTHING! When Gus and I go back down, we're gonna tag-team Justin Bieber's bowl cut!
Then he'll crash his Ferrari again.

L.A. Rain

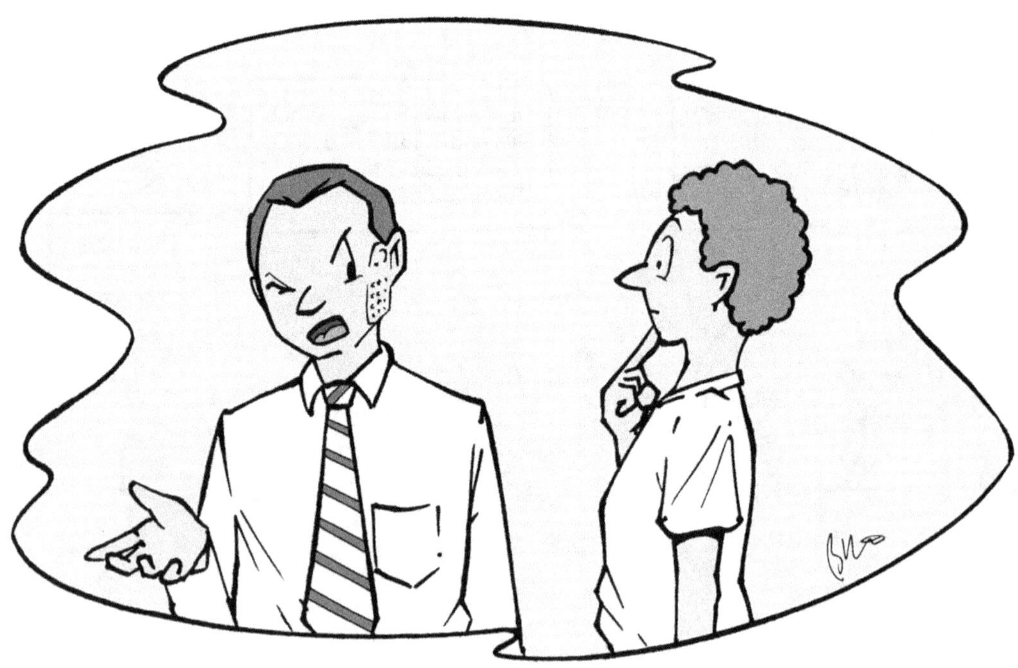

"Of course I use my cell phone a lot...why do you ask?"

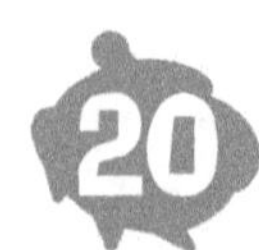

The Big "H"

HELLO??
HAPPY 4TH BIRTHDAY DA
BRREEEEEE...
?
SPACEMAN SPIFFY RAY GUN
HELLO?

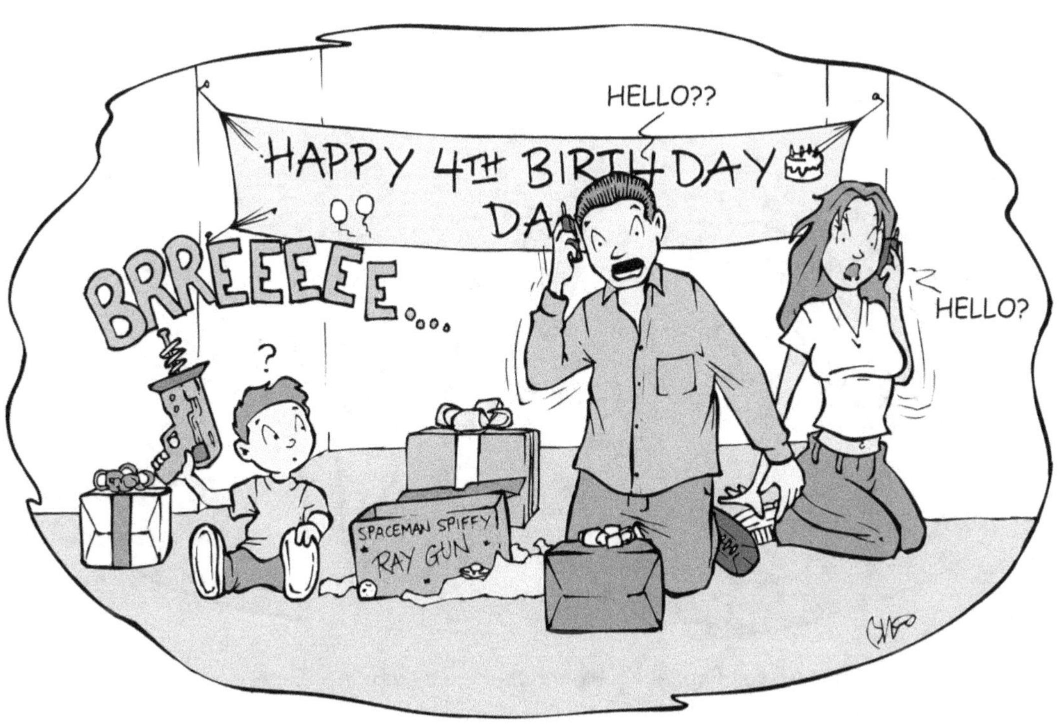

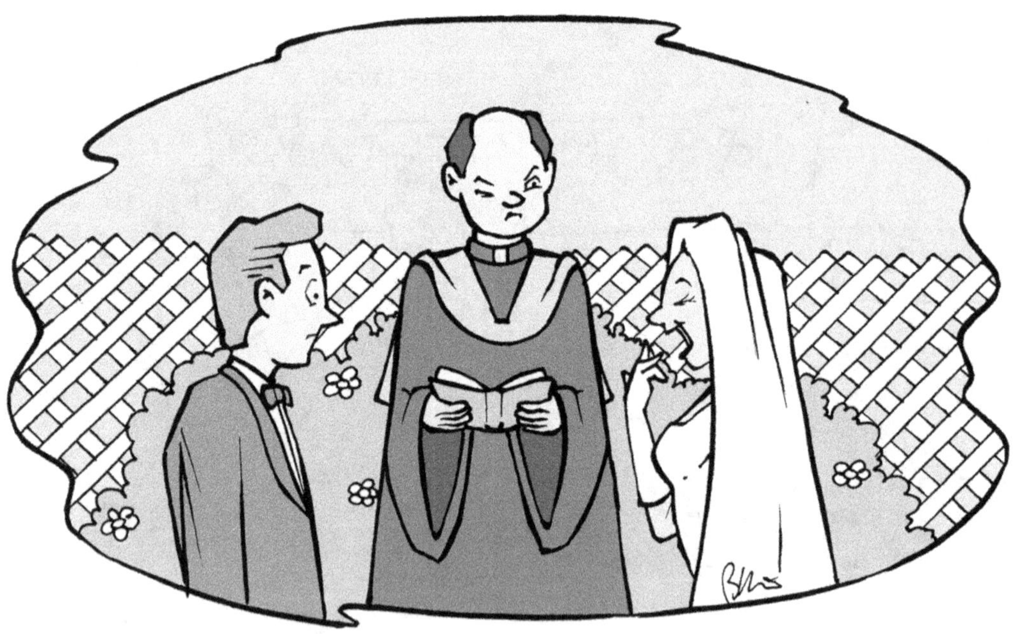

"For Richer or for Poorer?" Hahahahah....er....ahem.., I mean, "I do."

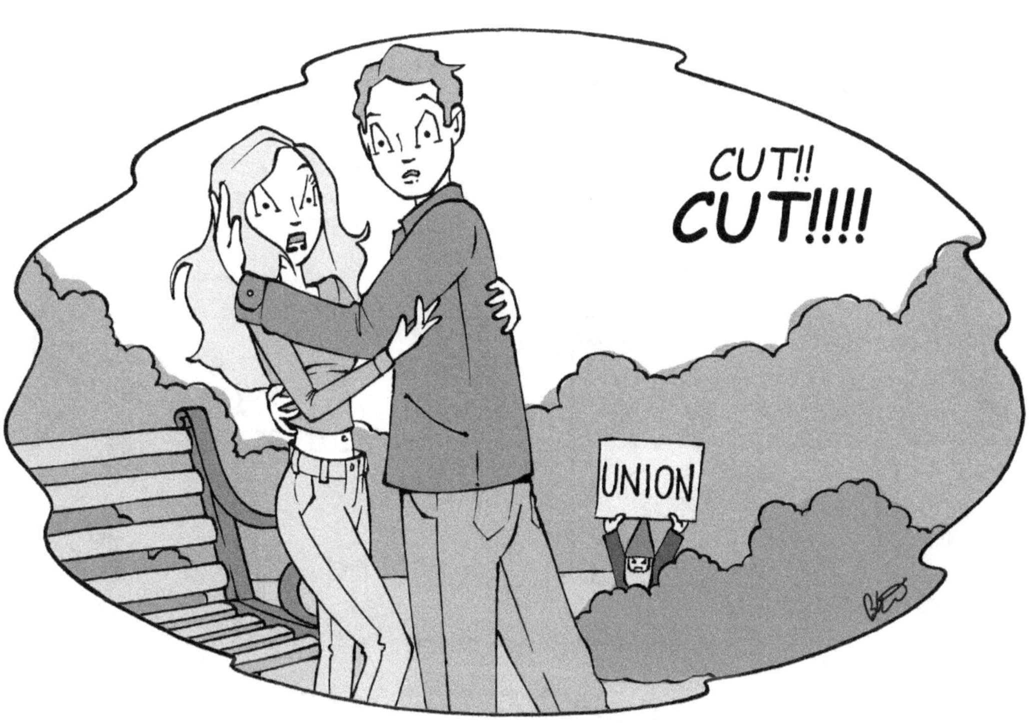
CUT!!
CUT!!!!
UNION

The Big "H"

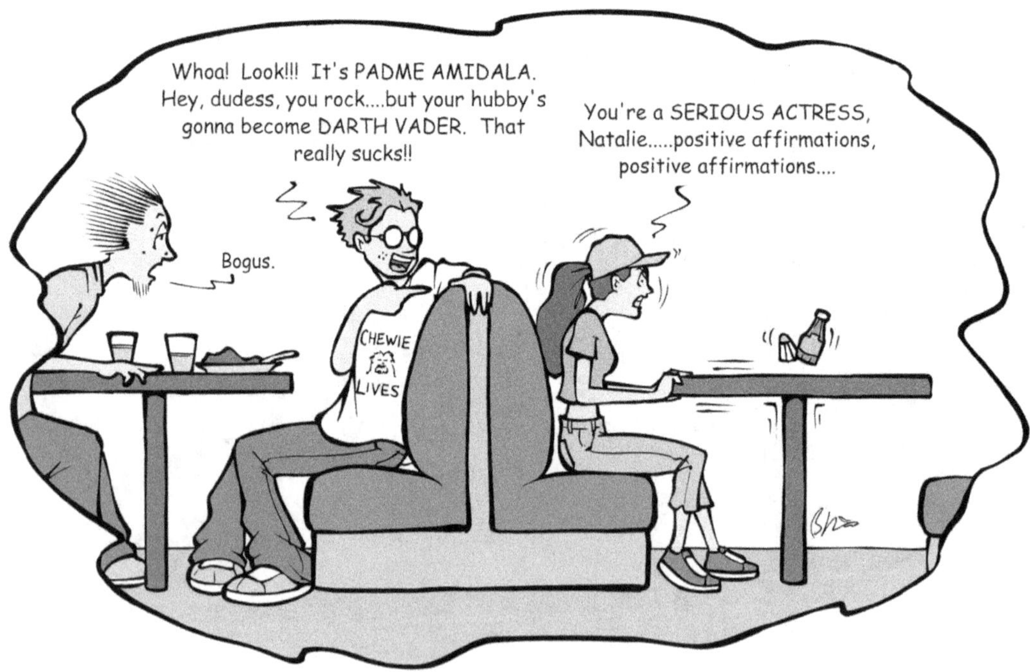
Bogus.
Whoa! Look!!! It's PADME AMIDALA. Hey, dudess, you rock....but your hubby's gonna become DARTH VADER. That really sucks!!
CHEWIE LIVES
You're a SERIOUS ACTRESS, Natalie.....positive affirmations, positive affirmations....

The Big "H"

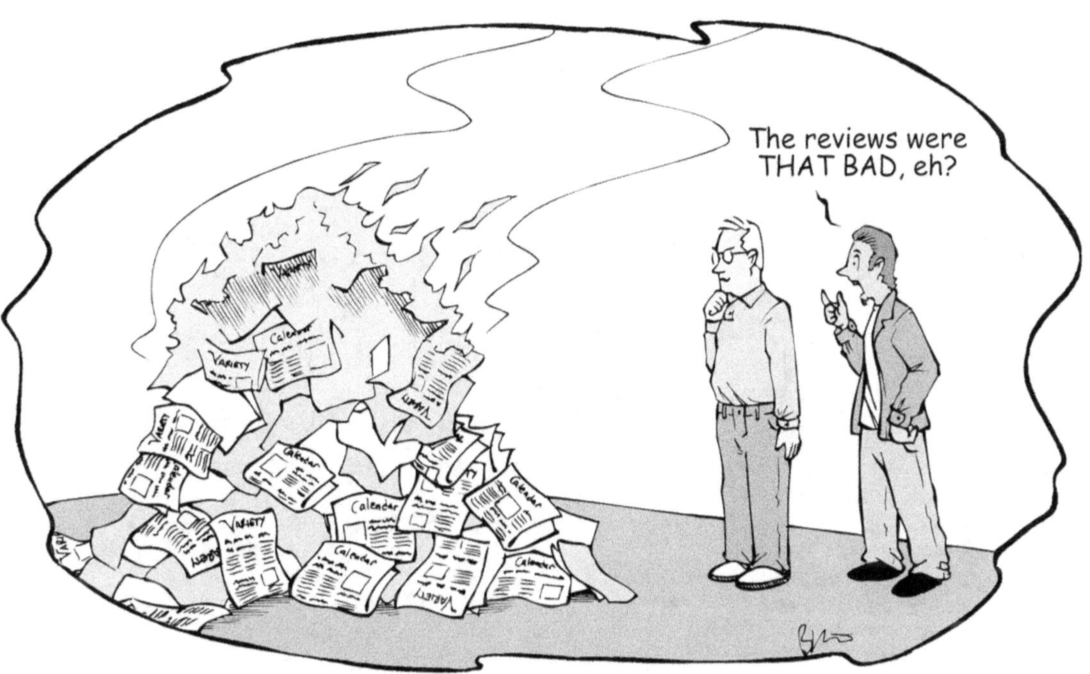

The Big "H"

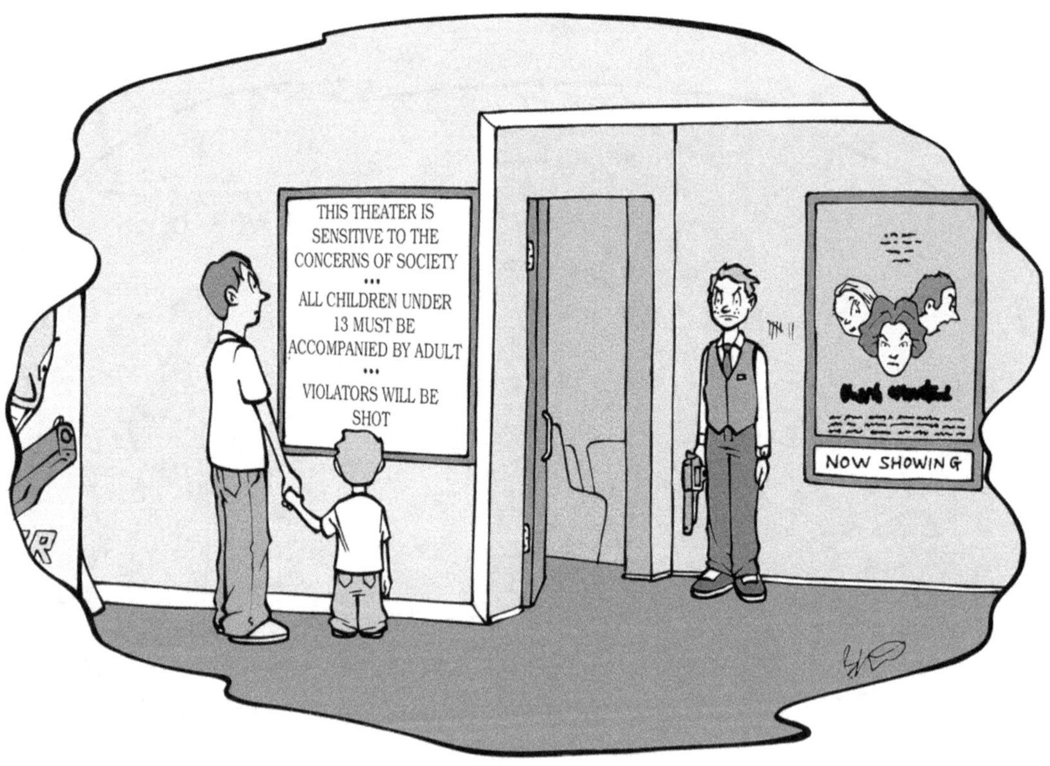
THIS THEATER IS SENSITIVE TO THE CONCERNS OF SOCIETY
•••
ALL CHILDREN UNDER 13 MUST BE ACCOMPANIED BY ADULT
•••
VIOLATORS WILL BE SHOT
NOW SHOWING

2. The "Bug" Strikes Again

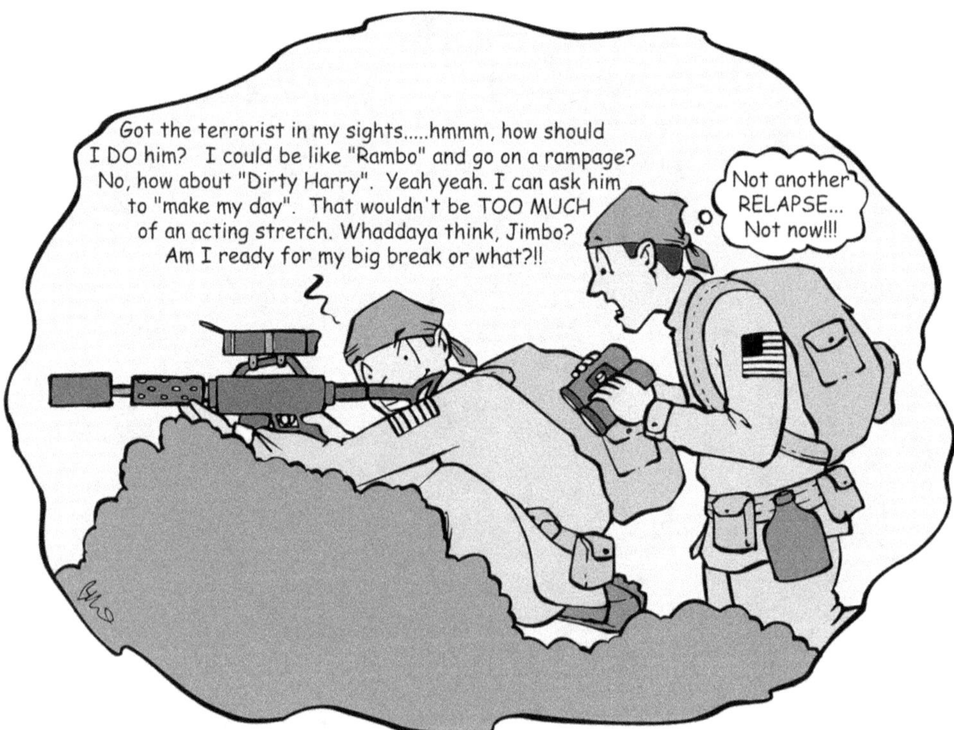

ACTOR'S ANONYMOUS -- DELTA FORCE CHAPTER

The Big "H"

NEW ARRIVALS
I ♥ LA
NEW ACTORS
OSCA
OR BUST
CROSS THE LINE
THE THEATRE IS
CLOSED

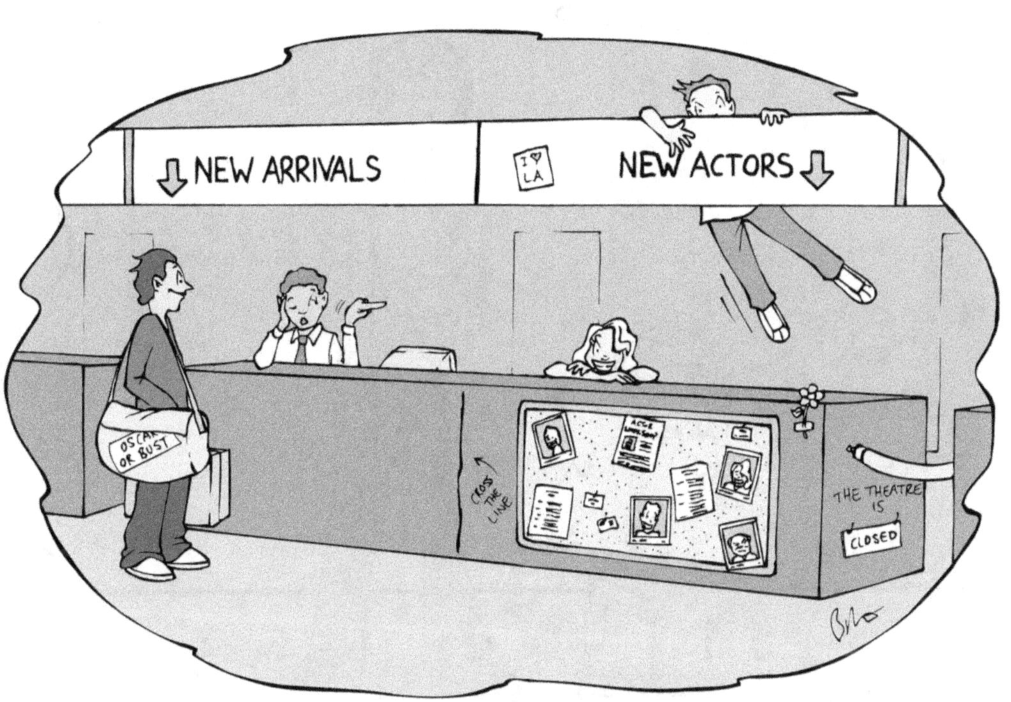

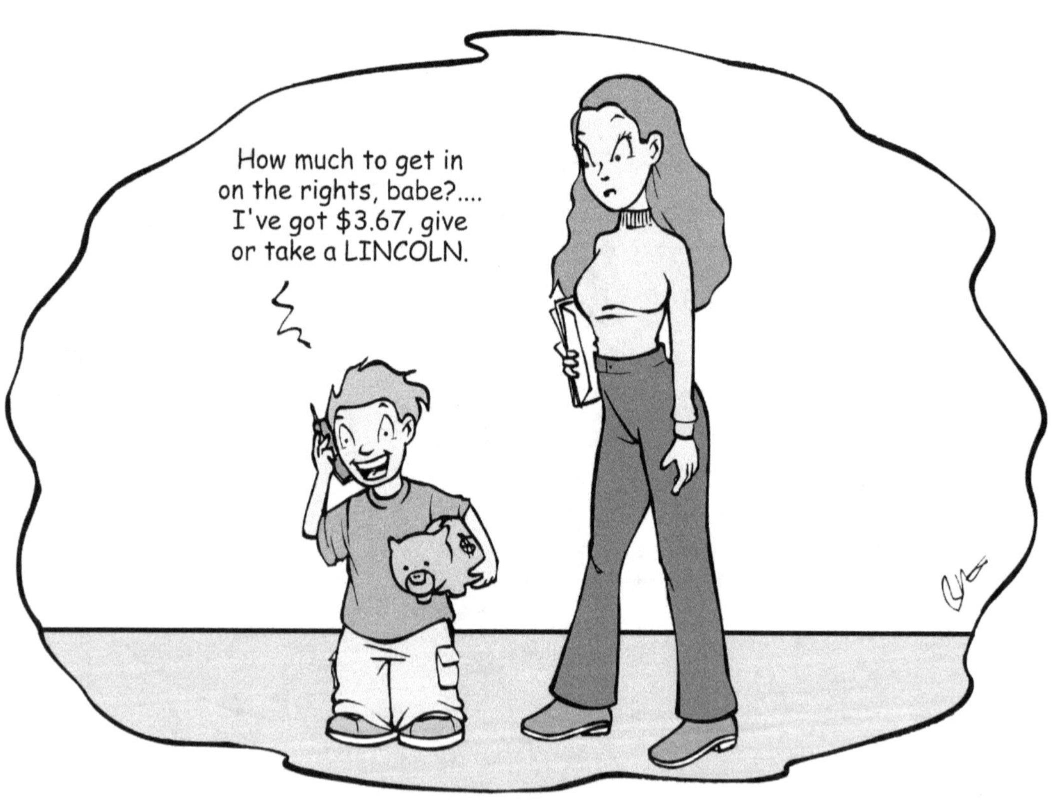
How much to get in
on the rights, babe?....
I've got $3.67, give
or take a LINCOLN.

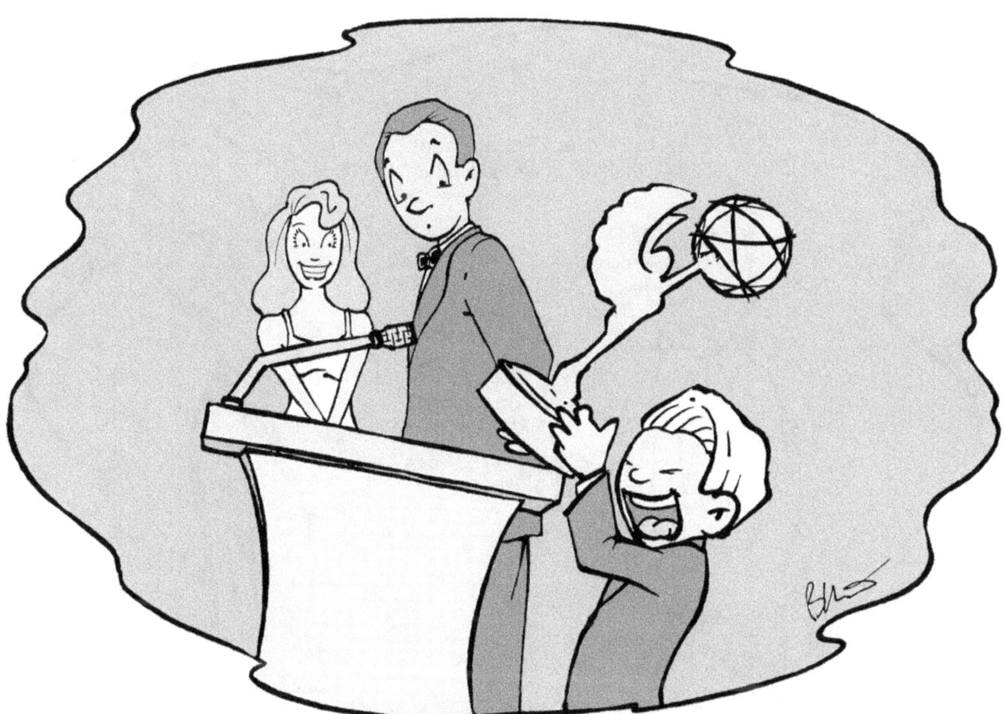

"I'd like to thank my parents, my friends, and Barney the Purple Dinosaur for helping me through those times when I didn't feel so special."

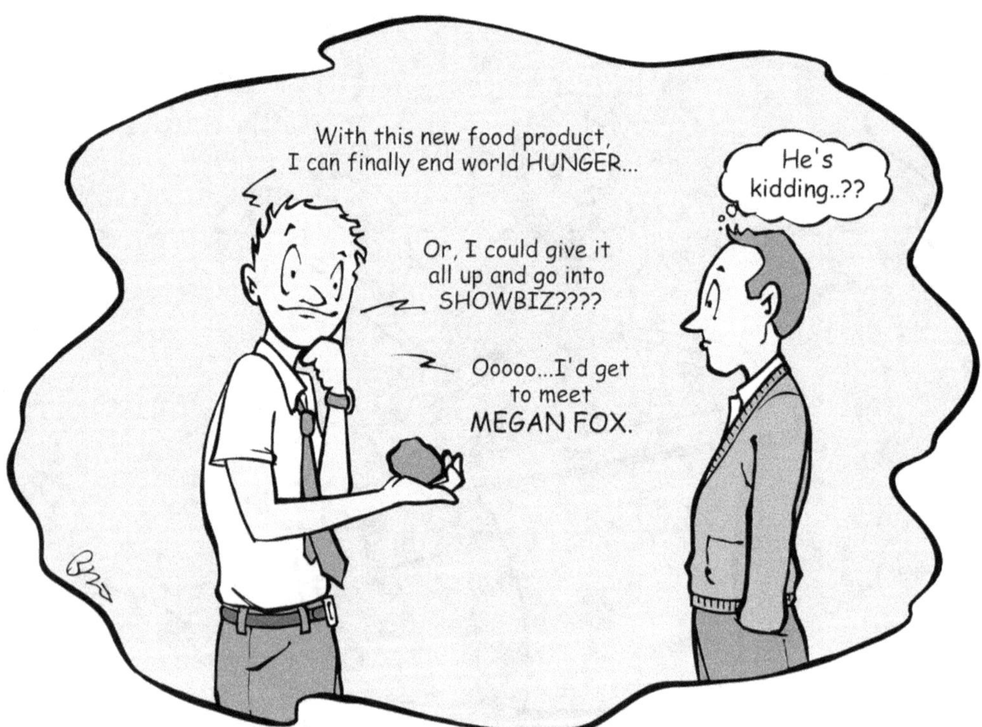

THE DANGERS OF STUDENT FILM CAMEOS...

The Big "H"

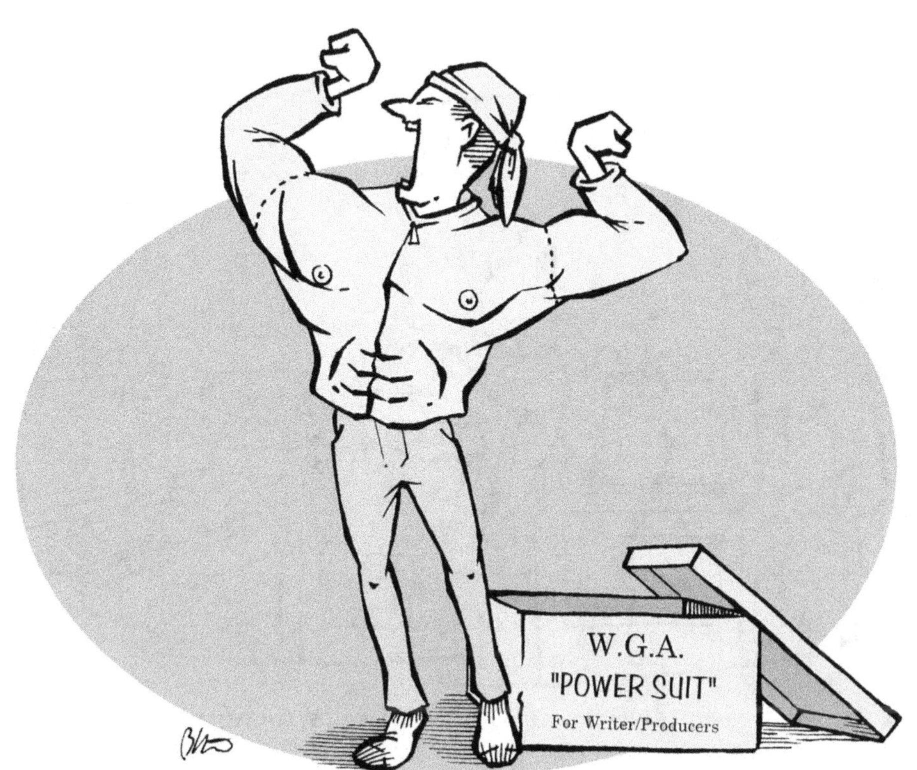

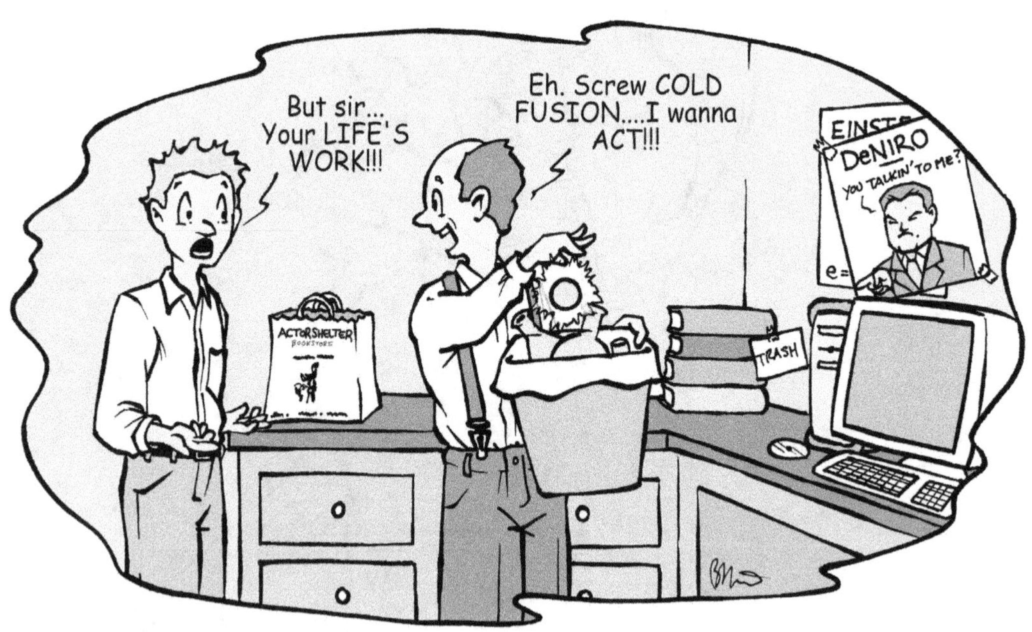

THE DANGERS OF STUDENT FILM CAMEOS...

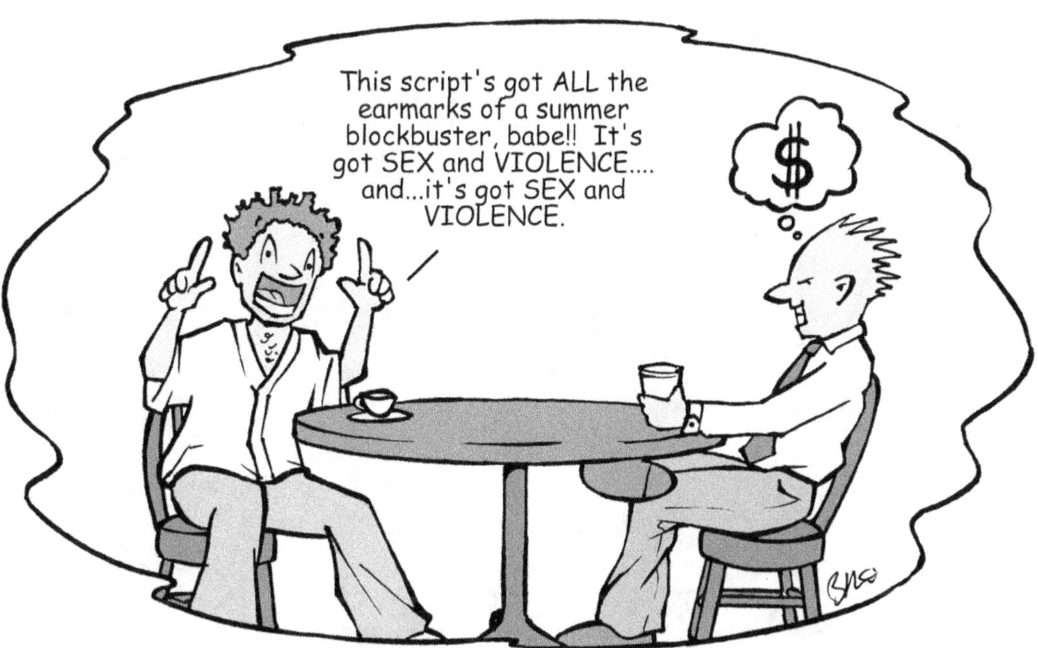

MOVER AND SHAKER (MOSHer)

The Big "H"

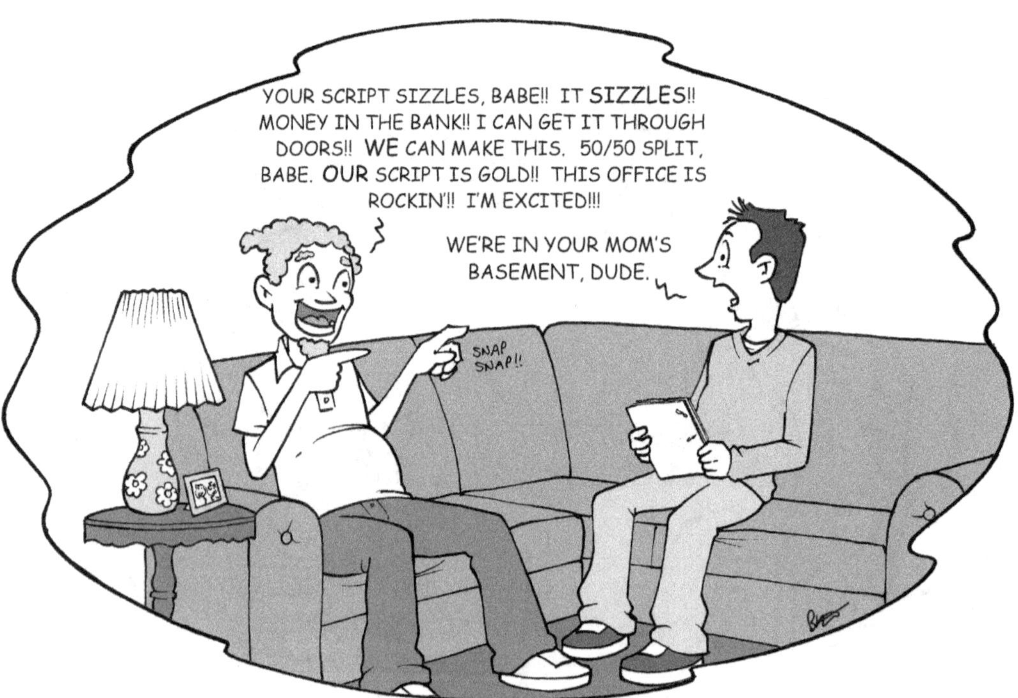

ATTACK OF THE MOSHER

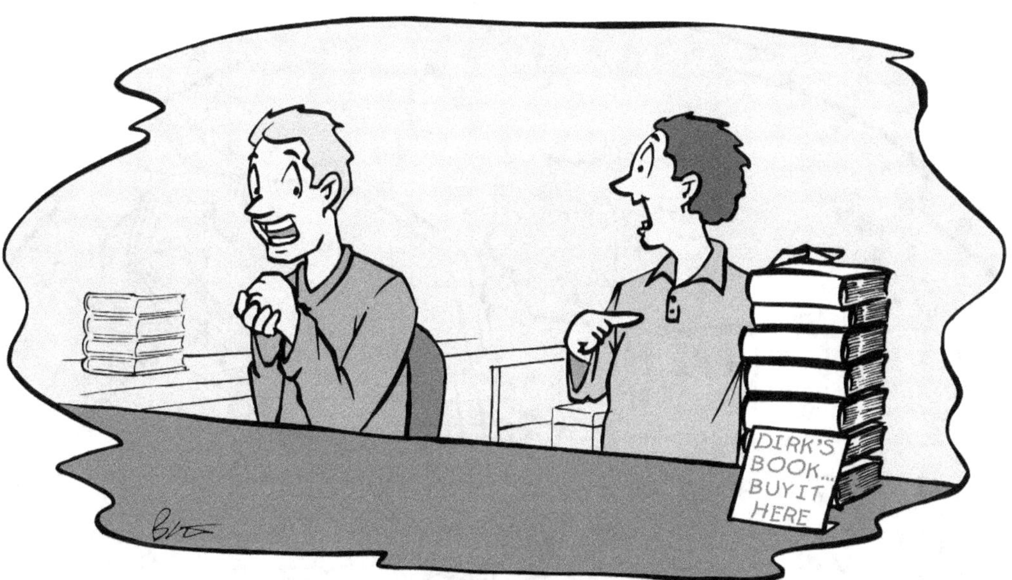

"Don't be silly, sir. You're a fine actor. There'll be a crowd over here in no time to grab themselves a signed copy of your new autobiography. I can feel the buzz already... by the way, we're CLOSING in five minutes."

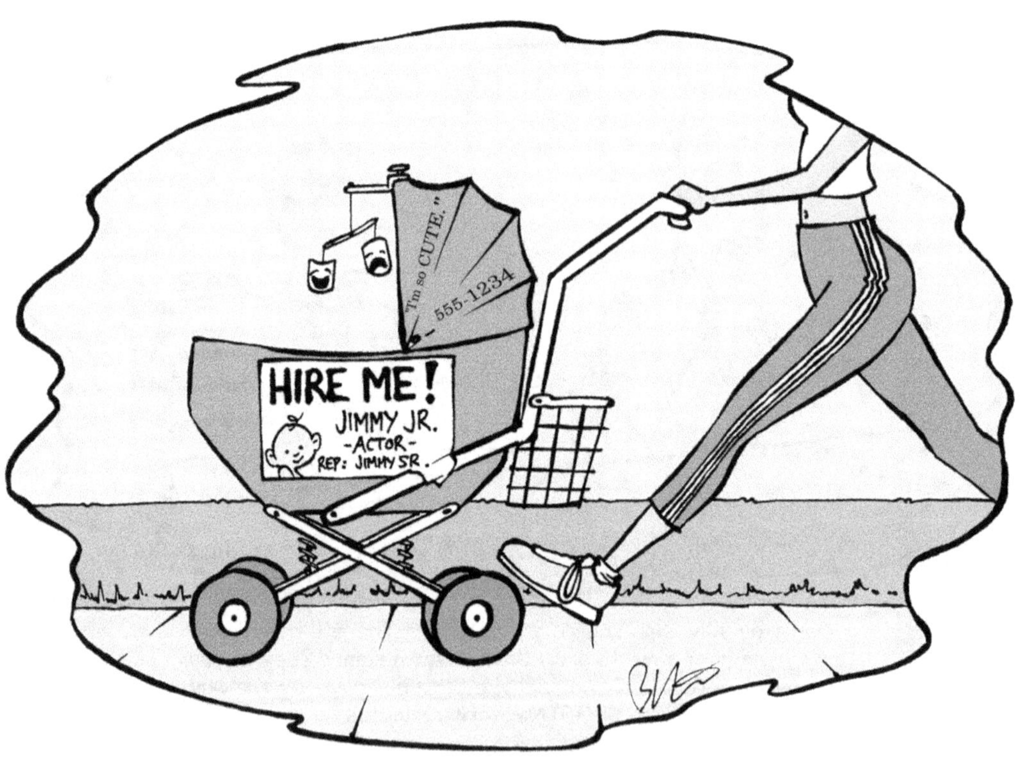
"I'm so CUTE."
555-1234
HIRE ME!
JIMMY JR.
-ACTOR-
REP: JIMMY SR.

The Big "H"

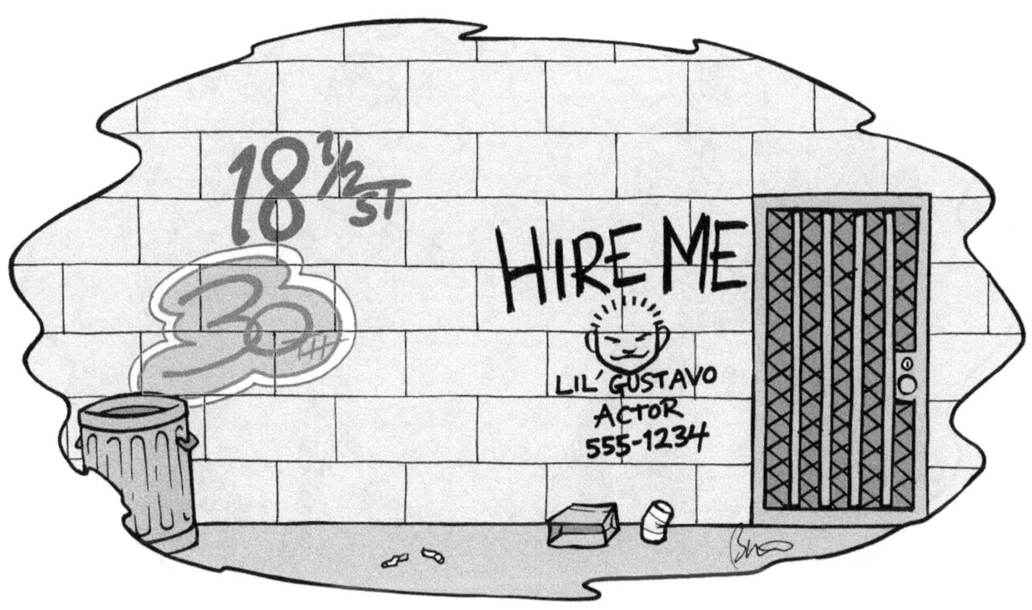

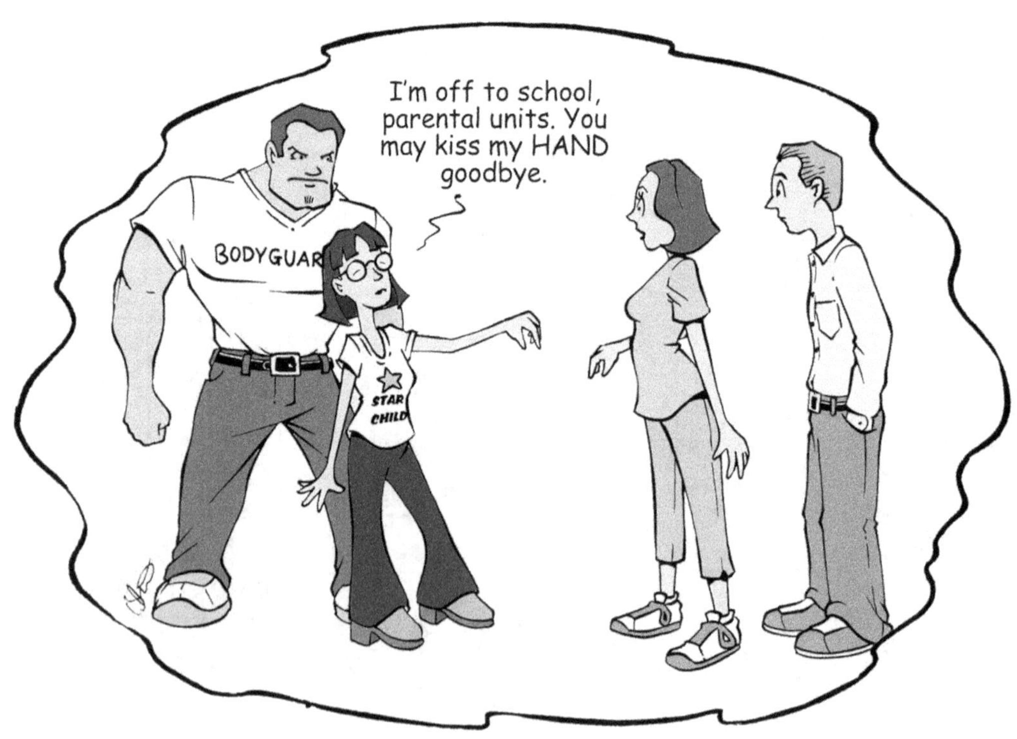

"SENIOR PRODUCTIONITIS"

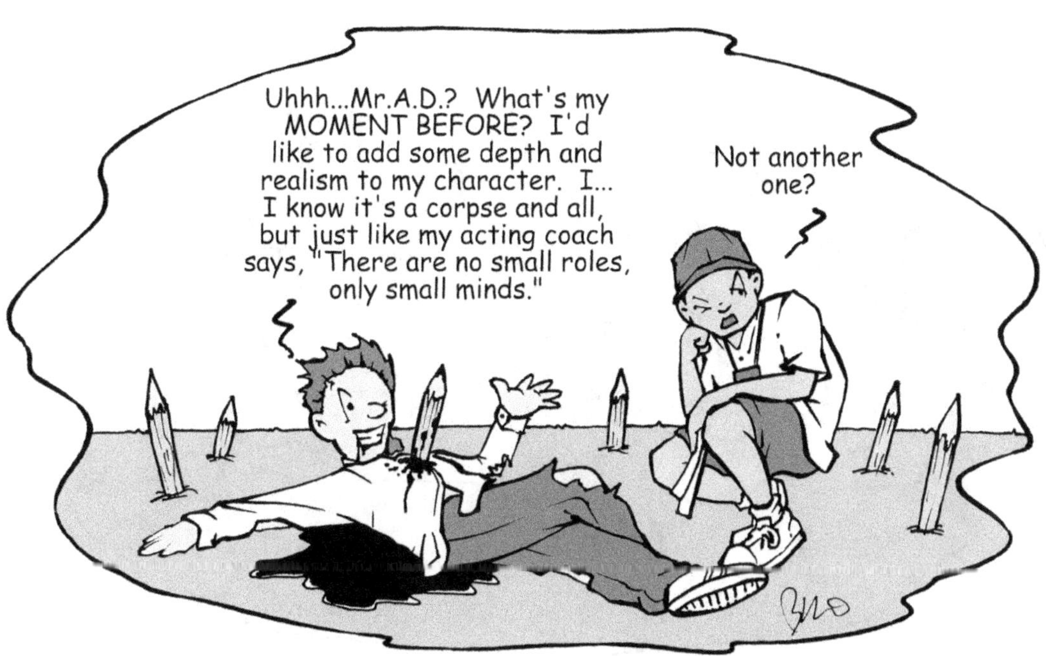
Uhhh...Mr.A.D.? What's my MOMENT BEFORE? I'd like to add some depth and realism to my character. I... I know it's a corpse and all, but just like my acting coach says, "There are no small roles, only small minds."
Not another one?

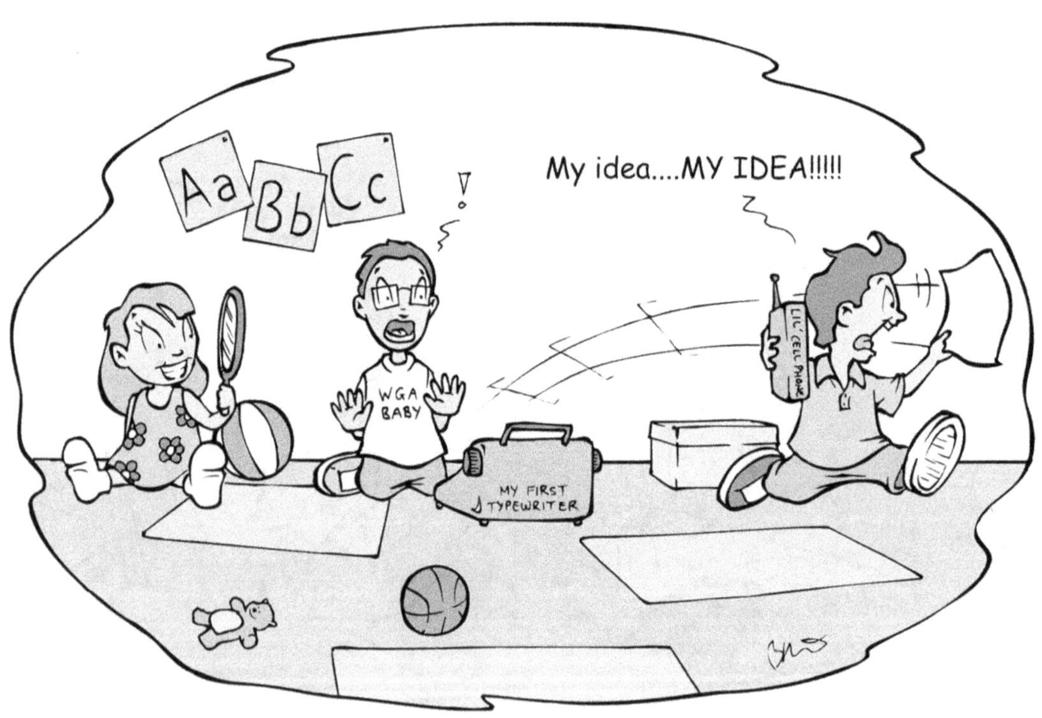

STUDIO DAY CARE MOSHER

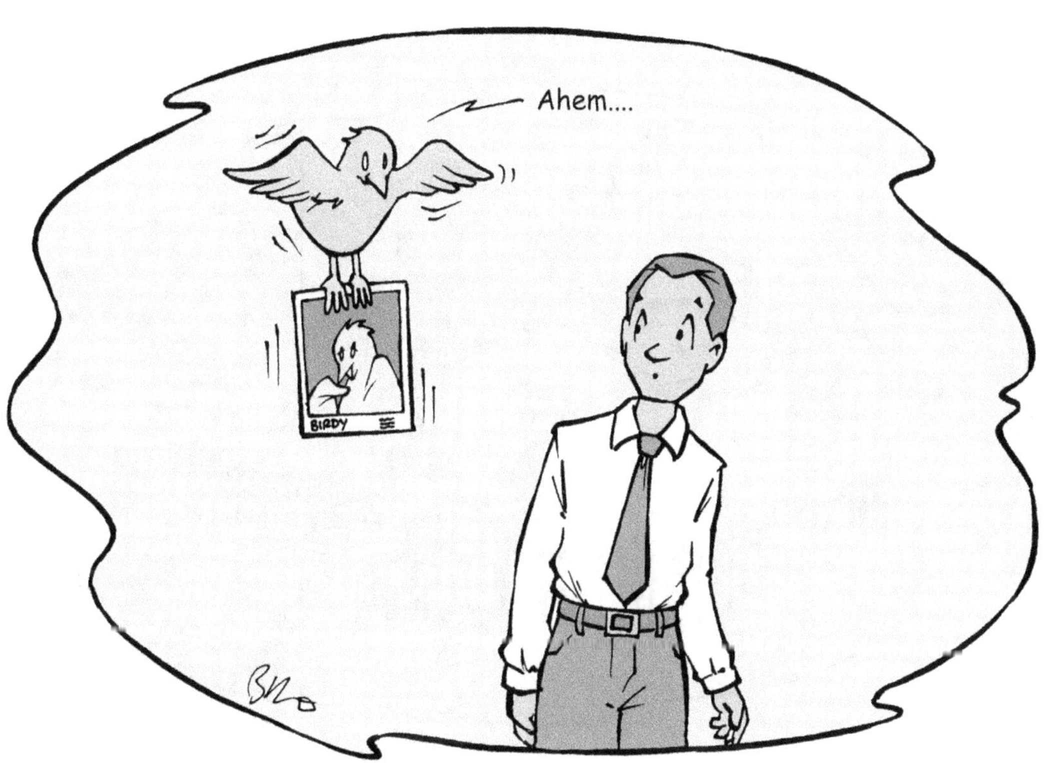
Ahem....
BIRDY

The Big "H"

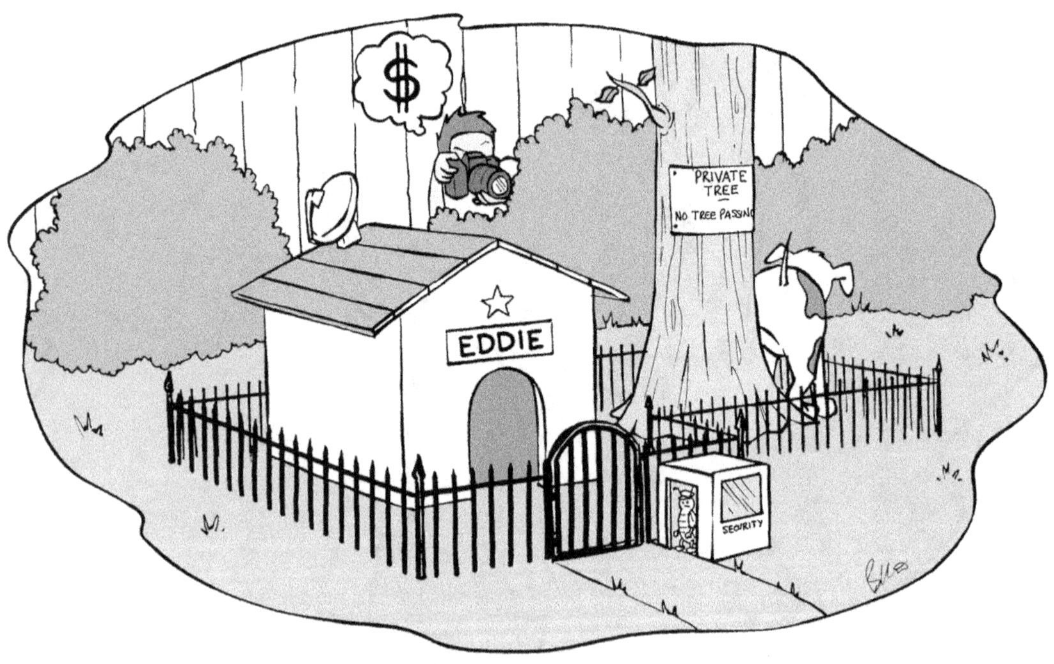

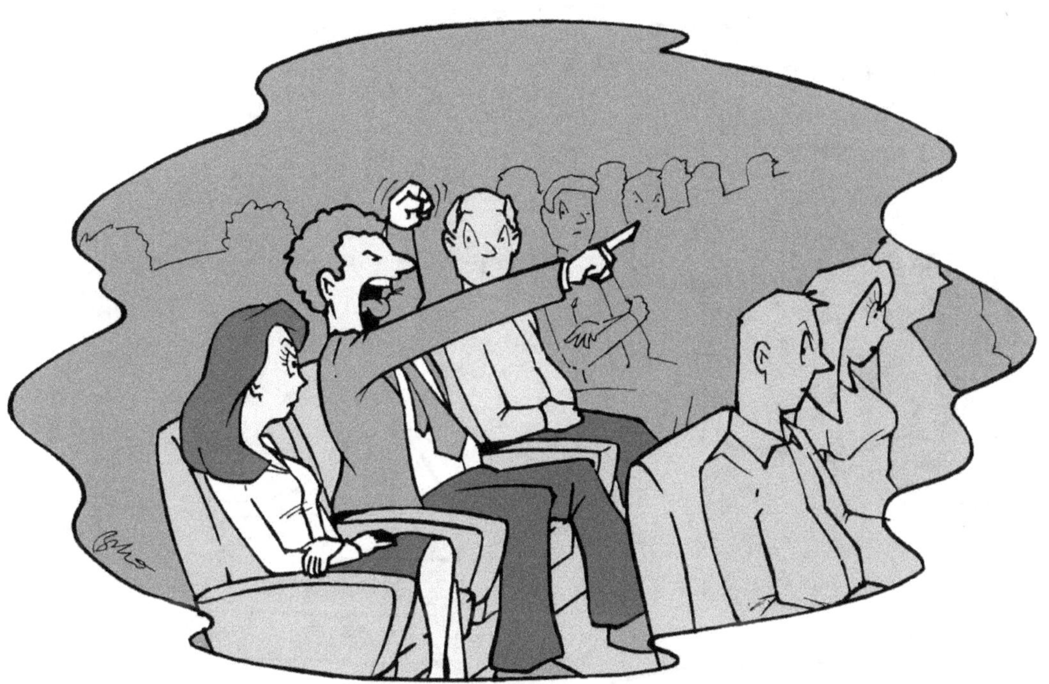

"WOOOO HOOOO!!! There I am, behind the counter!! Didja see me, didja see me? Yee haaaa!!!"

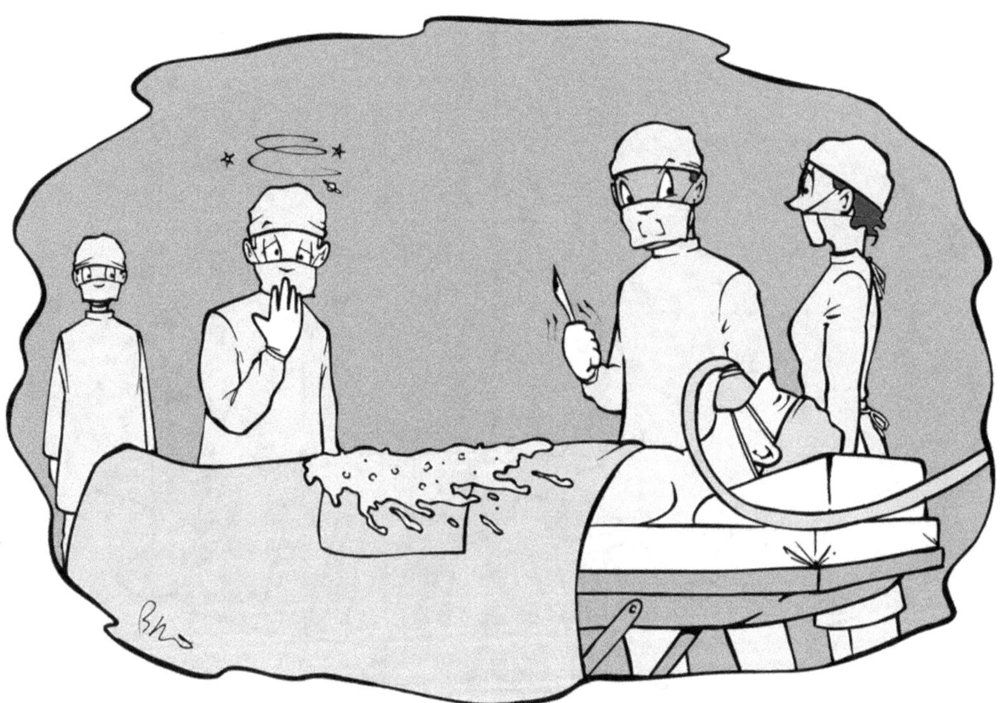

"'Oh, doctor. Let the cute actor in to see the surgery. He's doing research.....it'll be FUN.'"

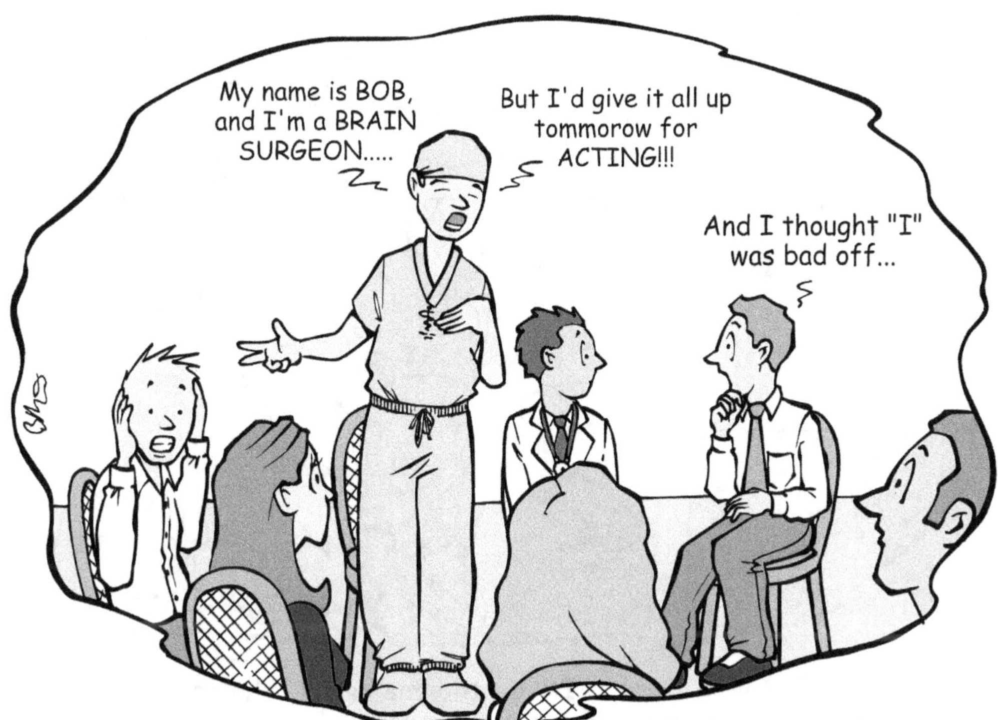

ACTORS ANONYMOUS -- $100,000+ SALARY CHAPTER...

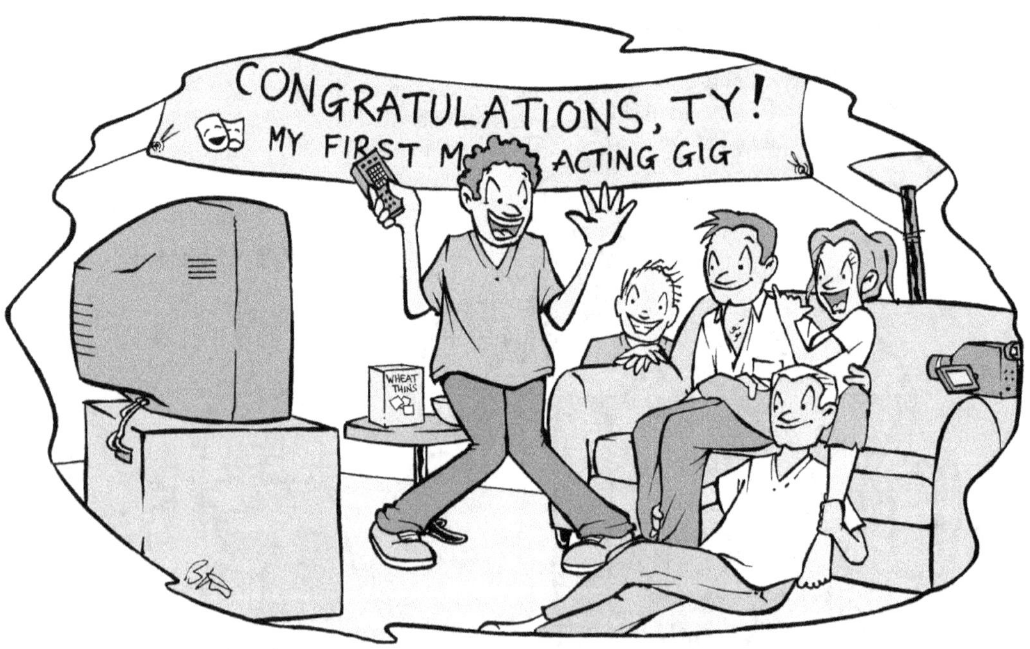

Okay!!! Here it comes. I'll be the one behind the counter.
I'm taping it, so we can watch us over, and over, and over.....

3. For The 5th Time...

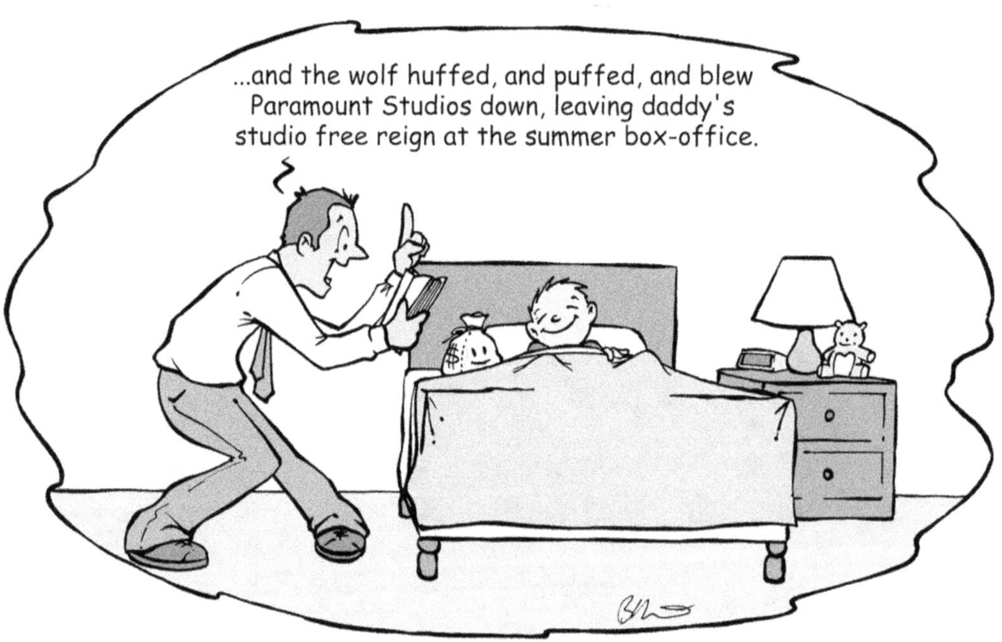

STUDIO BOSS BEDTIME STORY

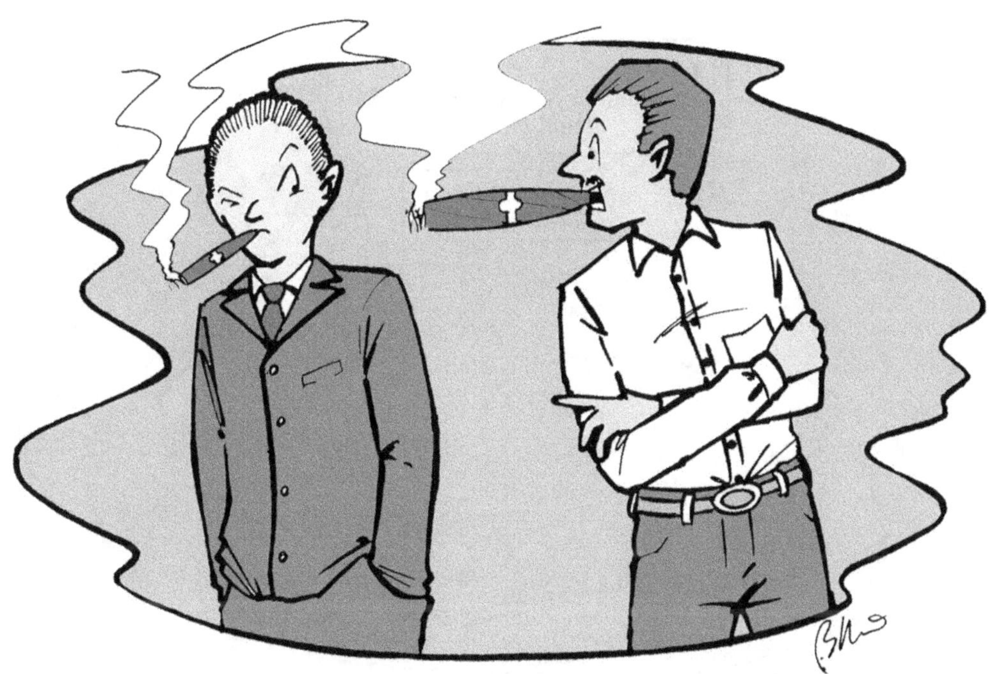

"Hey...looky here -- an ASSOCIATE PRODUCER!"

The Big "H"

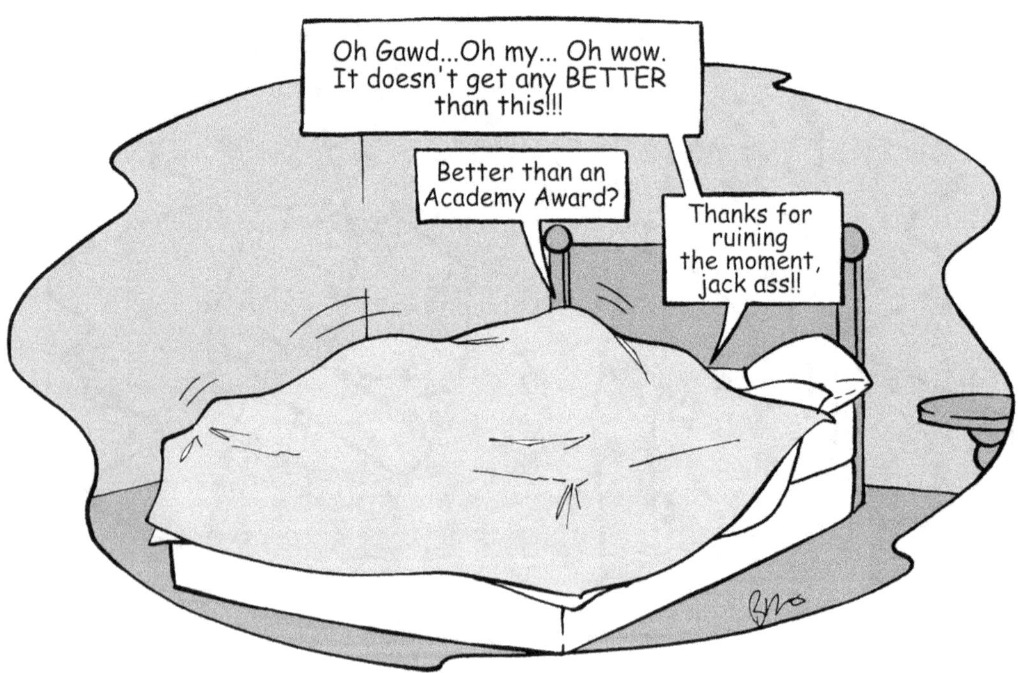

Oh Gawd...Oh my... Oh wow. It doesn't get any BETTER than this!!!
Better than an Academy Award?
Thanks for ruining the moment, jack ass!!

The Big "H"

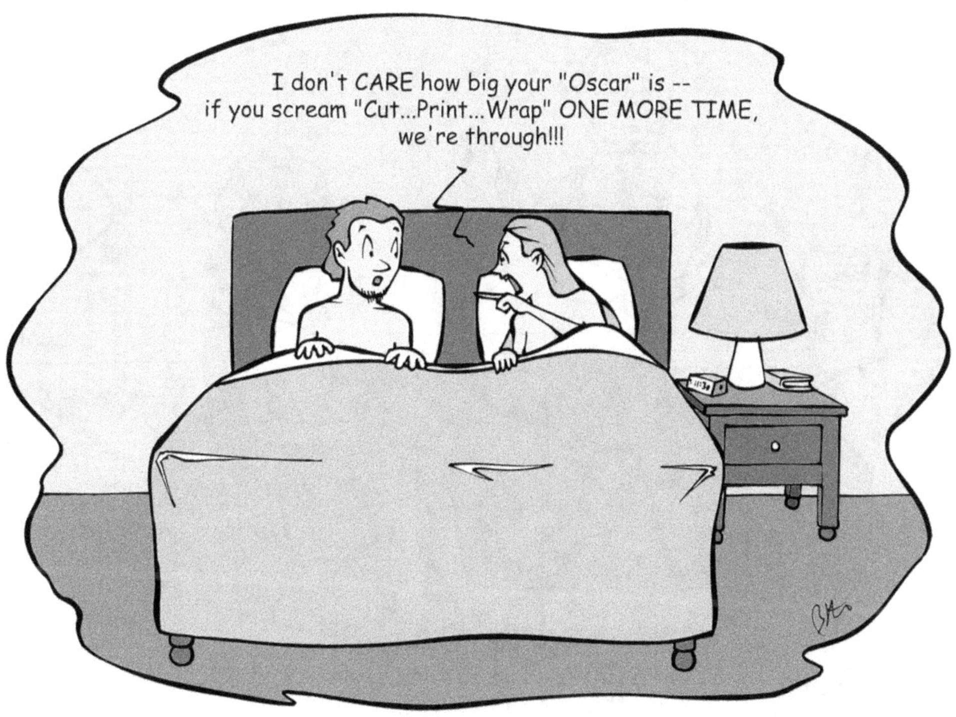
I don't CARE how big your "Oscar" is -- if you scream "Cut...Print...Wrap" ONE MORE TIME, we're through!!!

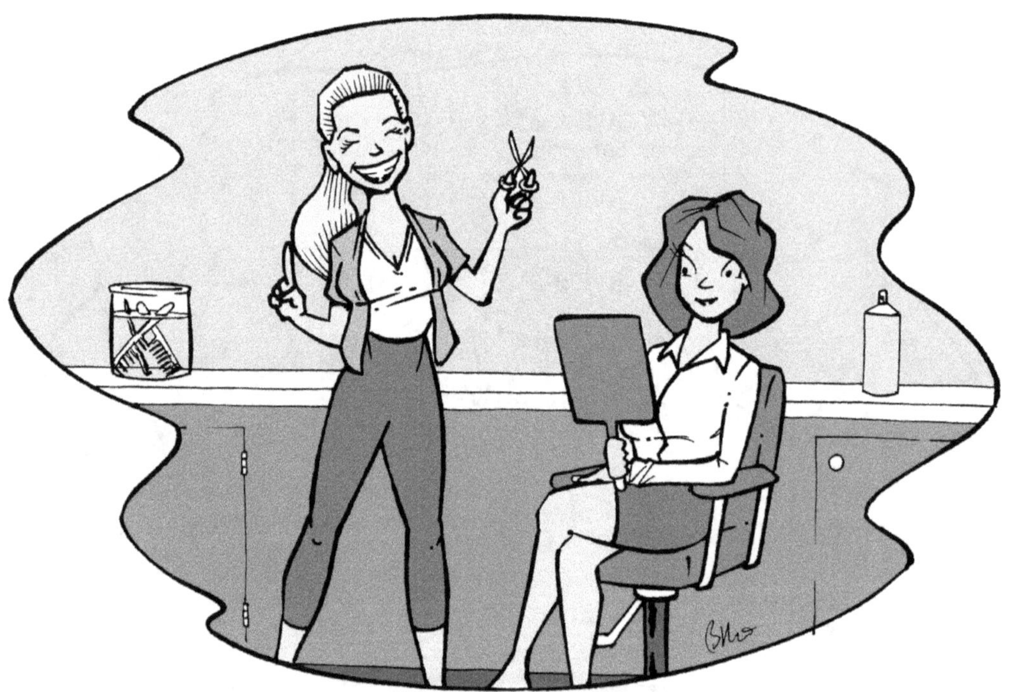

"Okay...that'll be $150 for the cut and style -- and $400 for the 'mental therapy'."

The Big "H"

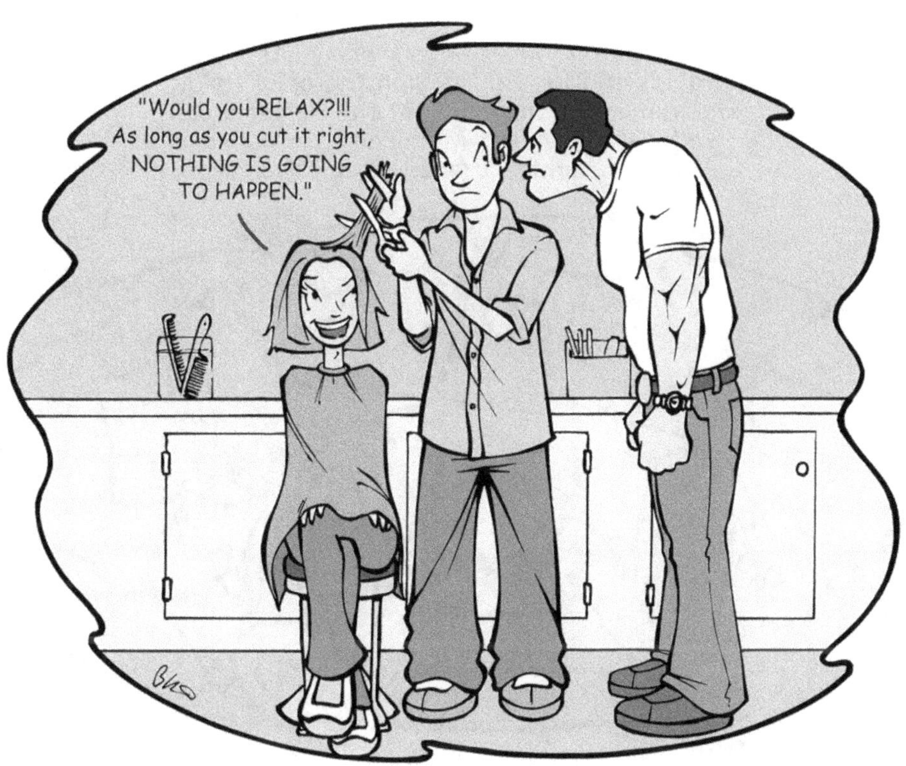
"Would you RELAX?!!! As long as you cut it right, NOTHING IS GOING TO HAPPEN."

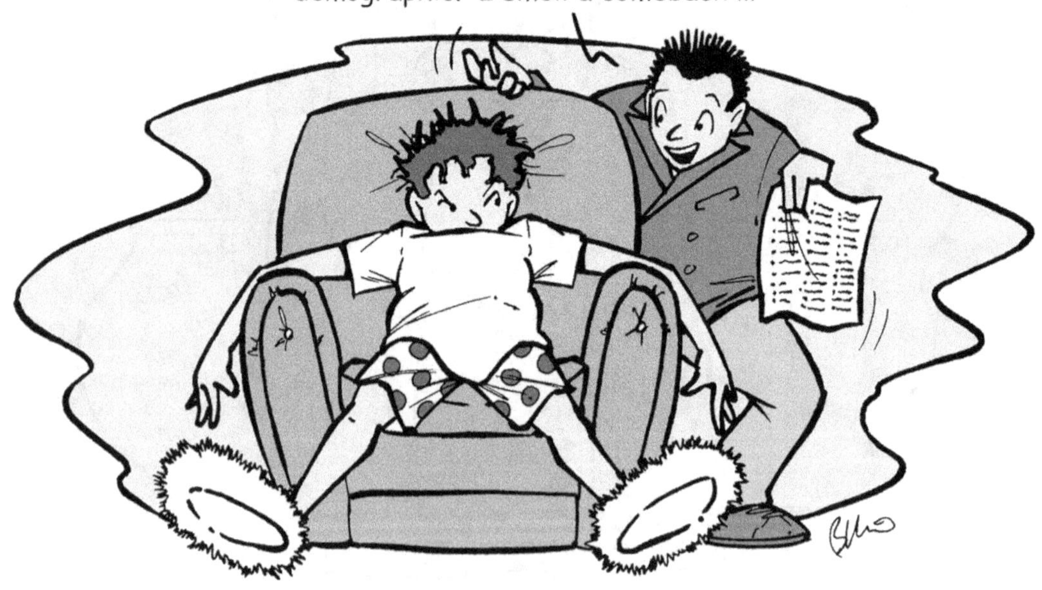
Okay...the bad news -- your show debuted at #134 out of 136. But look on the bright side -- we're number one amongst the out-of-work, welfare-dependent Michigan auto workers demographic. I smell a comeback !!!

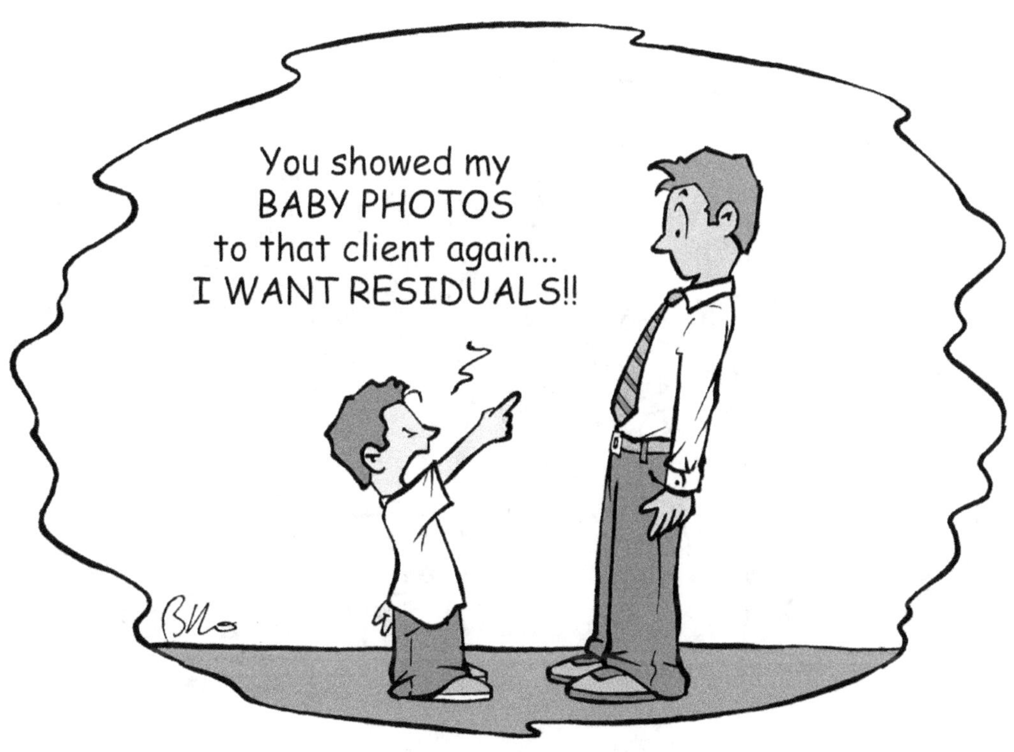
You showed my
BABY PHOTOS
to that client again...
I WANT RESIDUALS!!

S.A.G. BABY

The Big "H"

JUMBO
HOT DO
You guys again? There ARE other attractions here, y'know.
STAFF
HOUSE OF MIRRORS
ENTER HERE

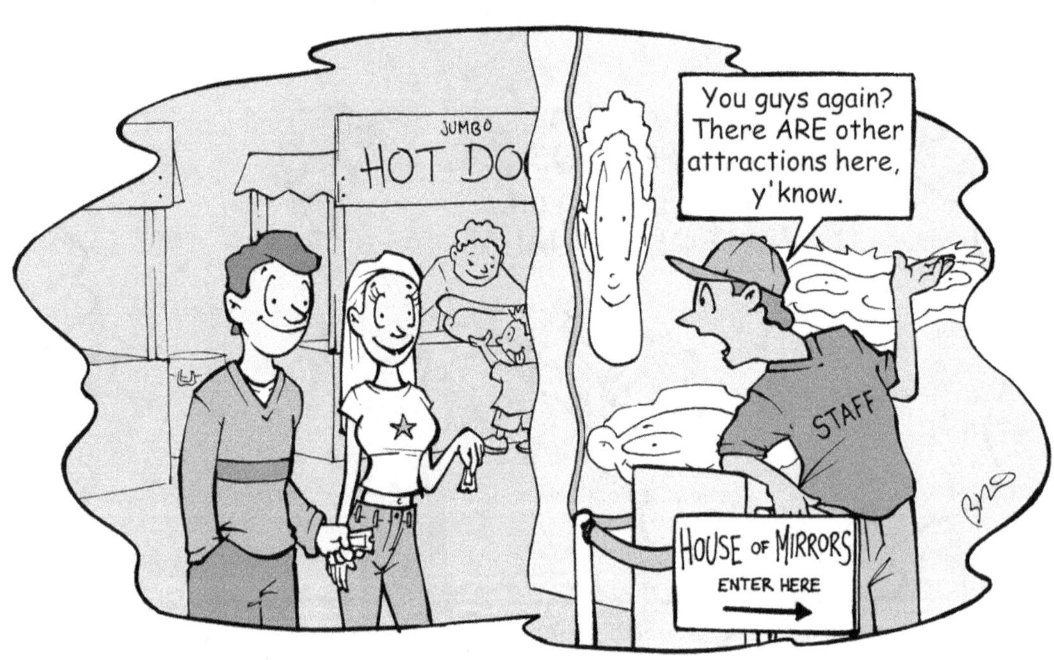

The Big "H"

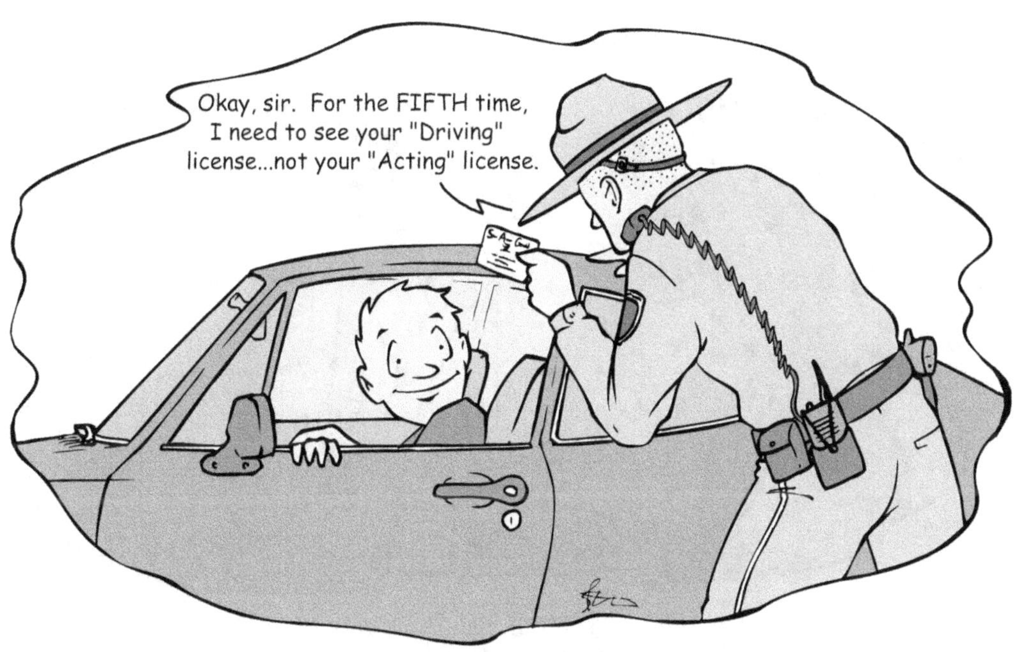

S.A.G. ROOKIE

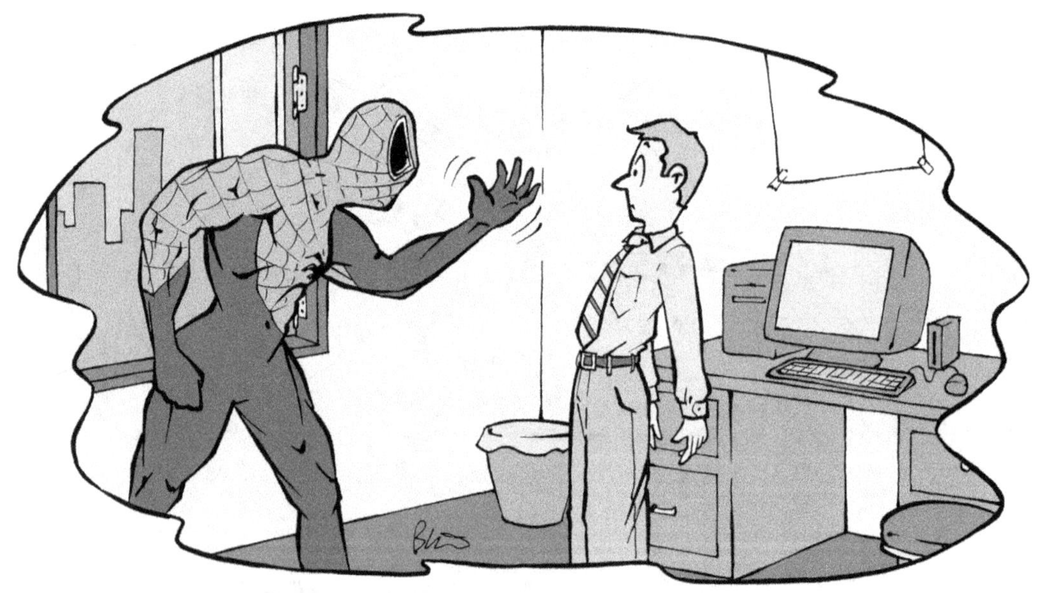

"For the LAST TIME, pal --- I don't build WEBSITES...now stop screaming for me!!!"

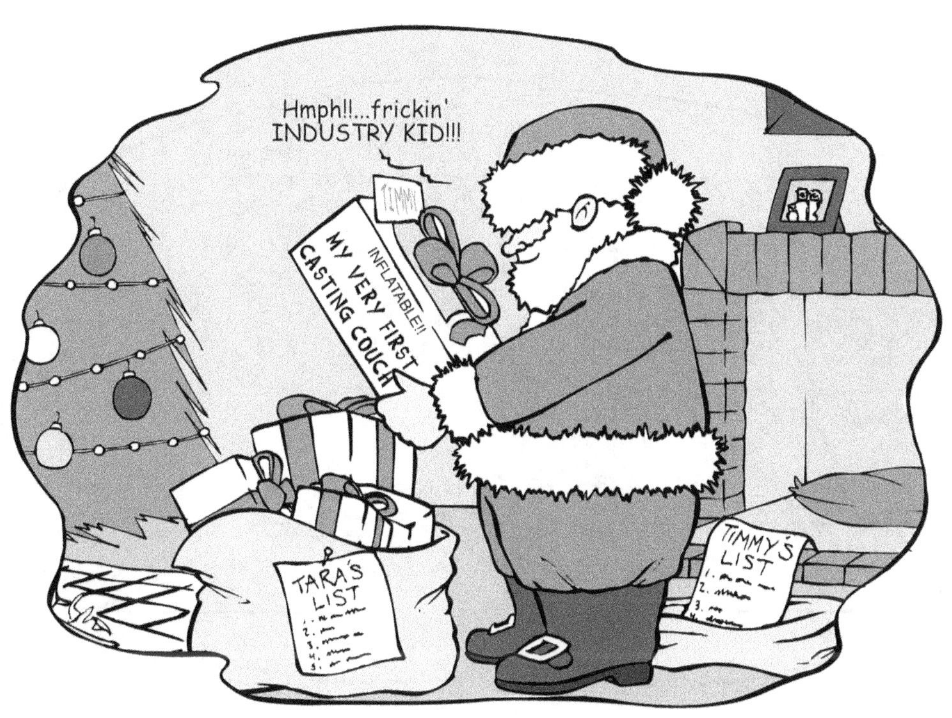
Hmph!!...frickin'
INDUSTRY KID!!!
TIMMY
INFLATABLE!!
MY VERY FIRST
CASTING COUCH
TARA'S LIST
TIMMY'S LIST

The Big "H"

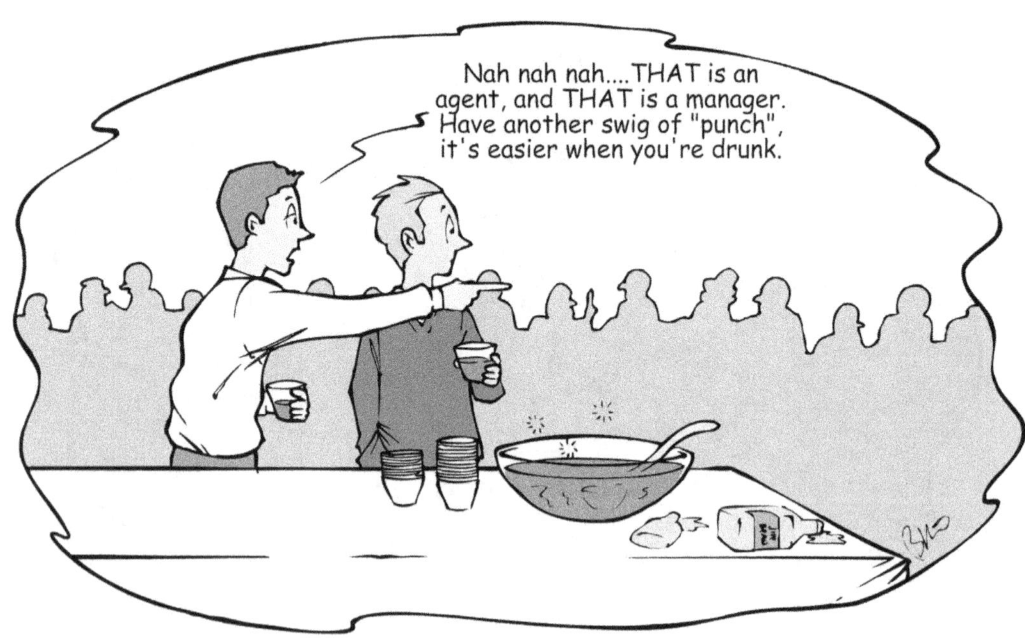
Nah nah nah....THAT is an agent, and THAT is a manager. Have another swig of "punch", it's easier when you're drunk.

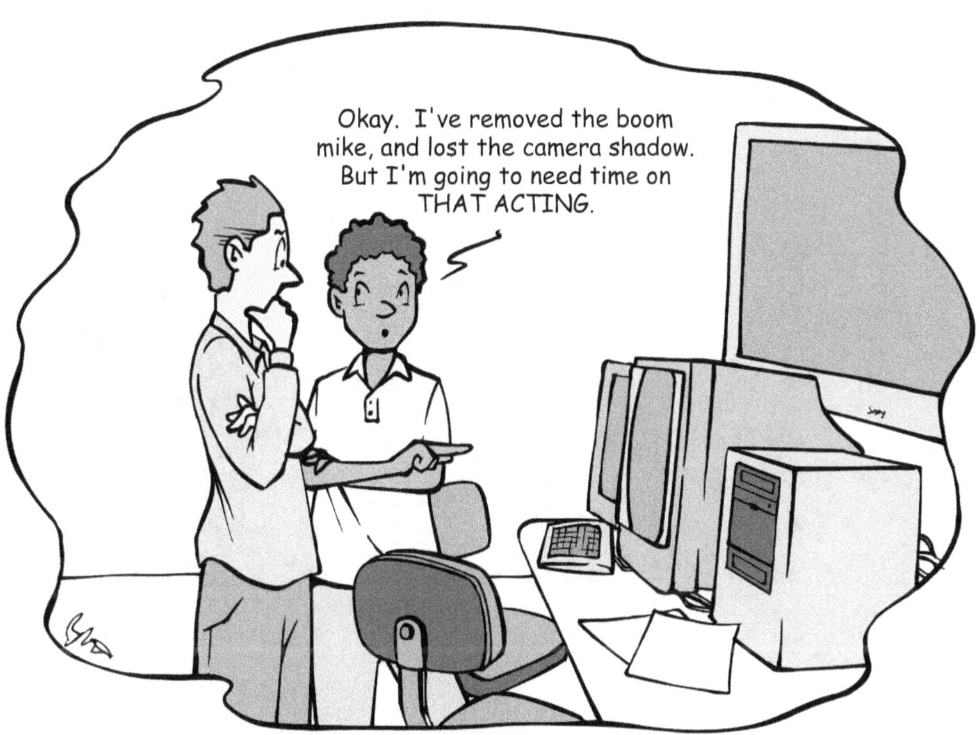

THE MIRACLE OF MODERN TECHNOLOGY

The Big "H"

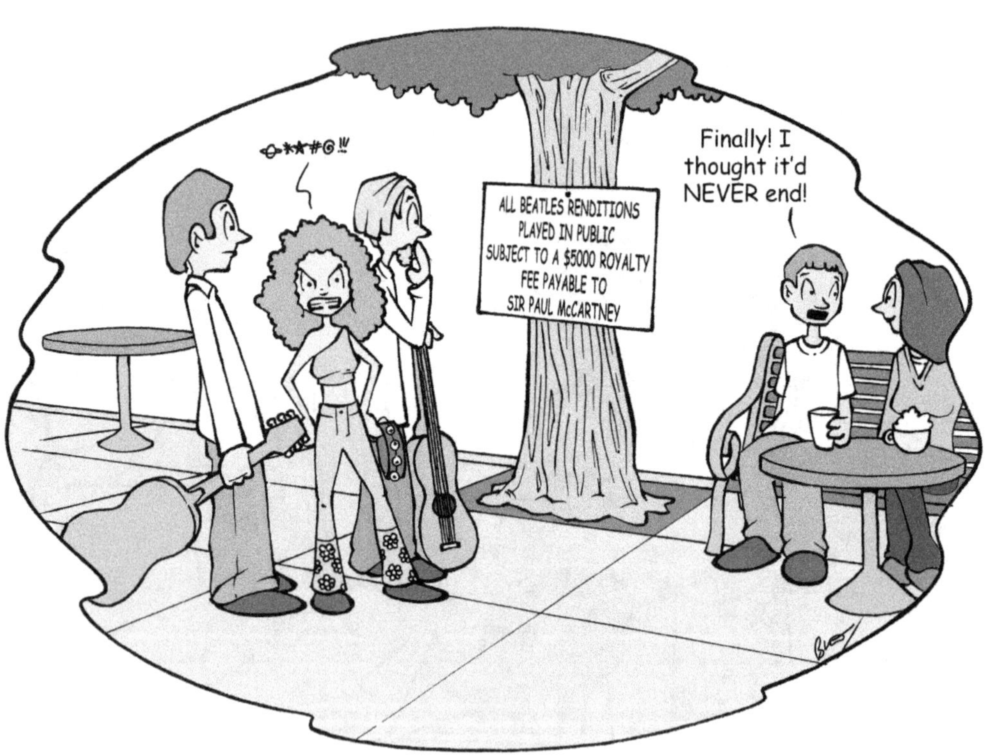

ALL BEATLES RENDITIONS PLAYED IN PUBLIC SUBJECT TO A $5000 ROYALTY FEE PAYABLE TO SIR PAUL McCARTNEY
Finally! I thought it'd NEVER end!

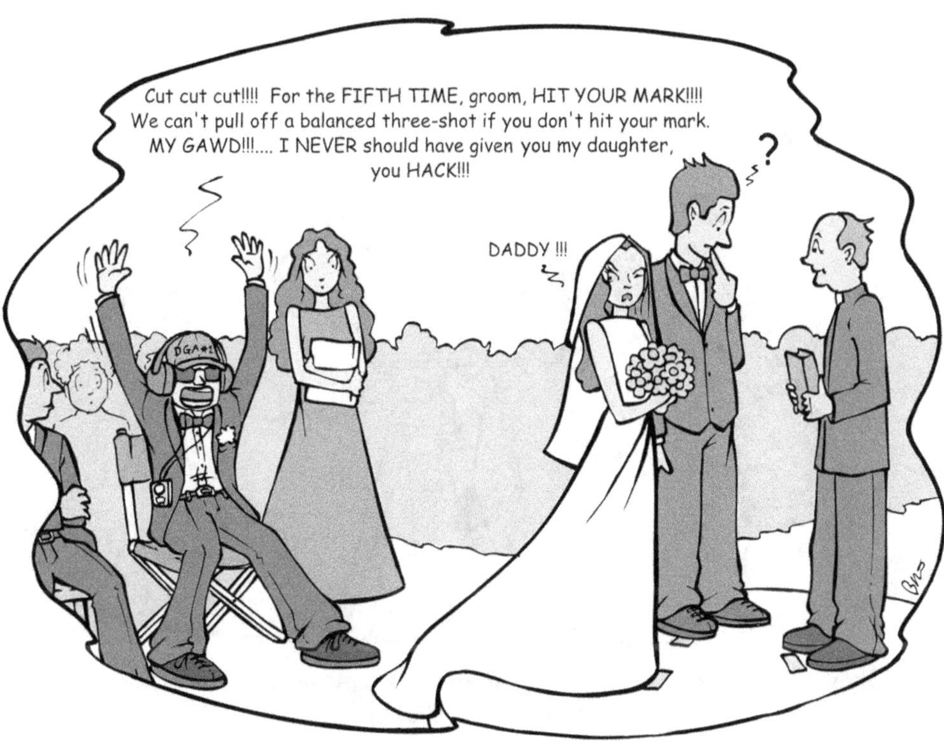

WEDDING DIRECTOR

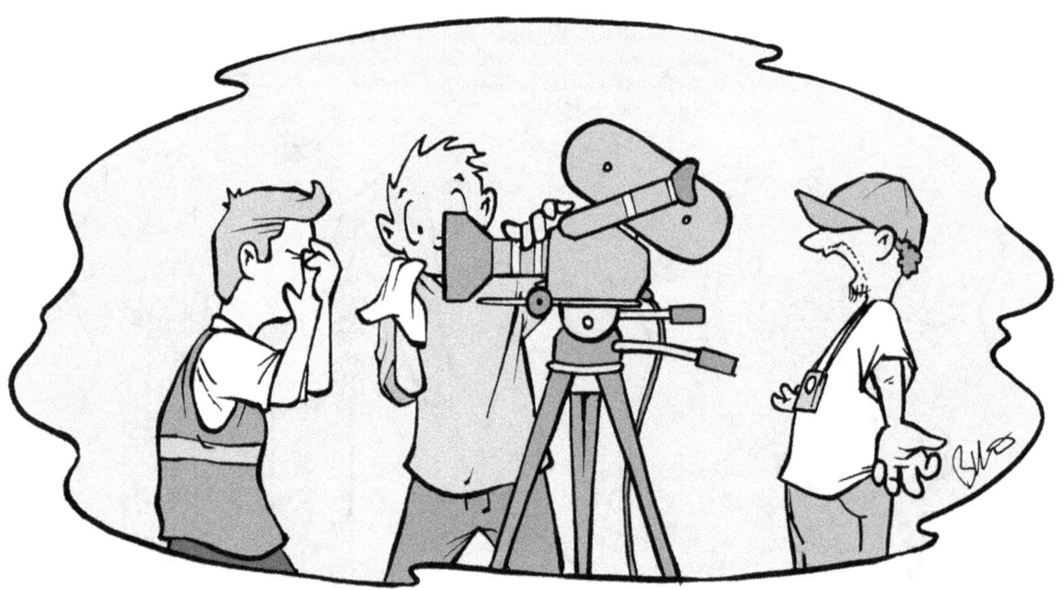

"Okay...for the FIFTH time -- when I say 'move in for a close-up', I don't mean YOU !!"

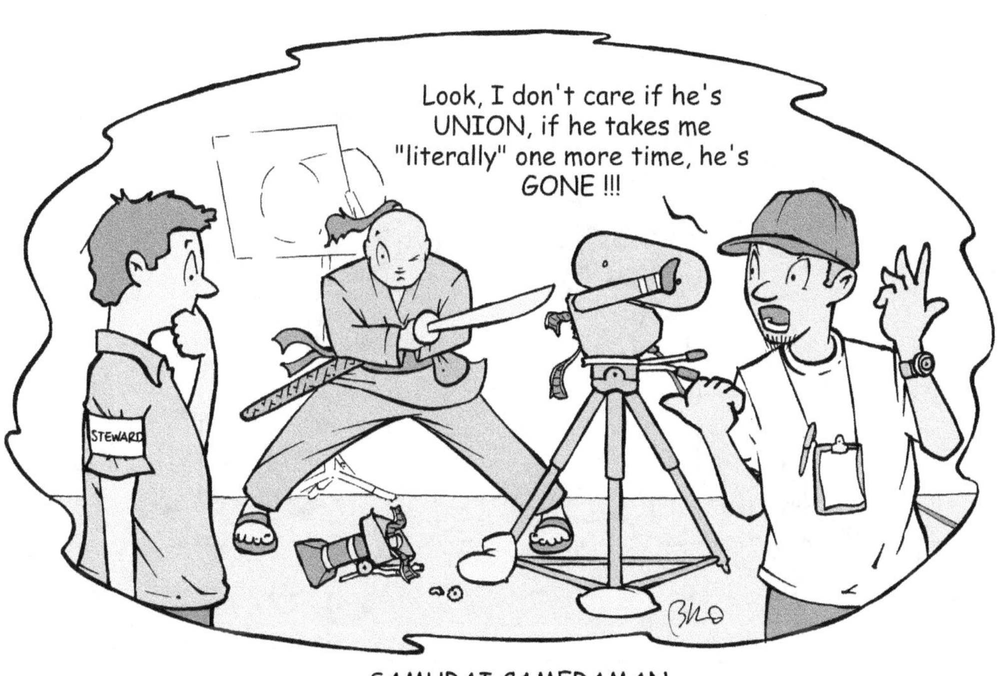

SAMURAI CAMERAMAN

The Big "H"

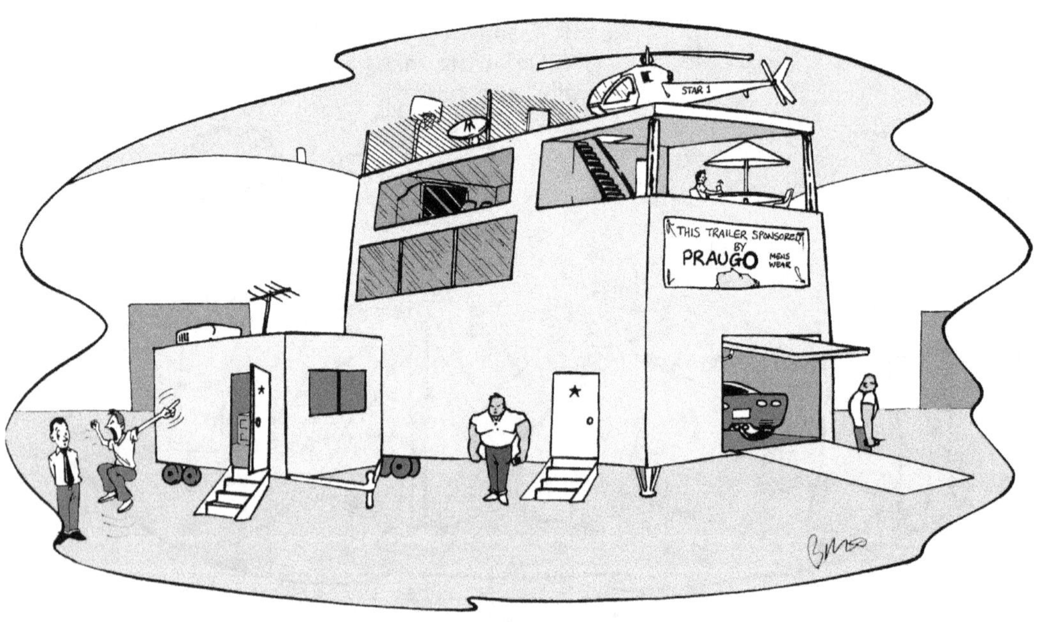

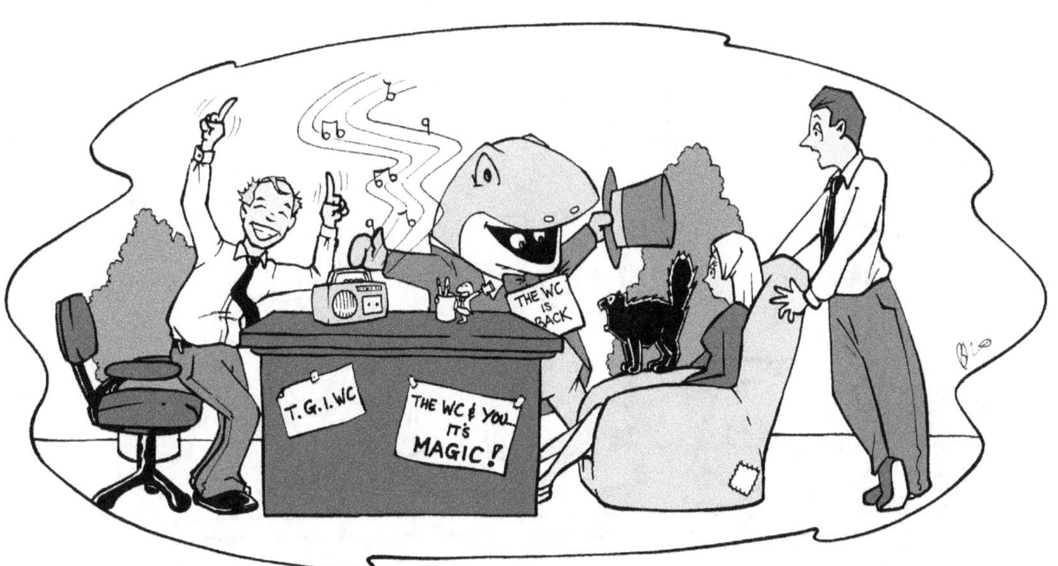

"I dunno about you, but I've gotta BAD FEELING about this."

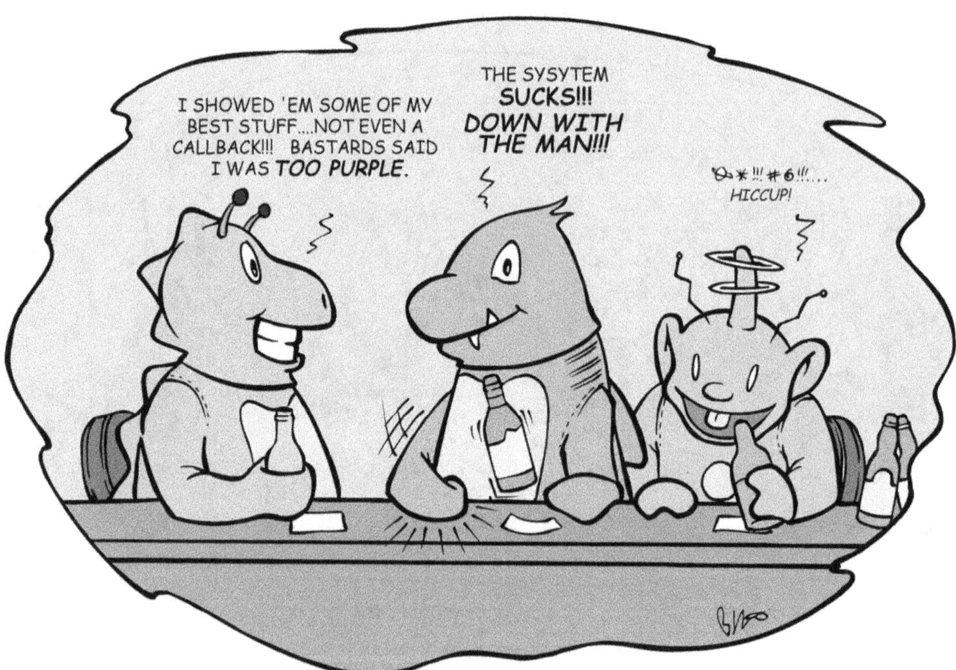

JADED KIDDIE SHOW CHARACTERS

4. The Lifestyle Section

The Big "H"

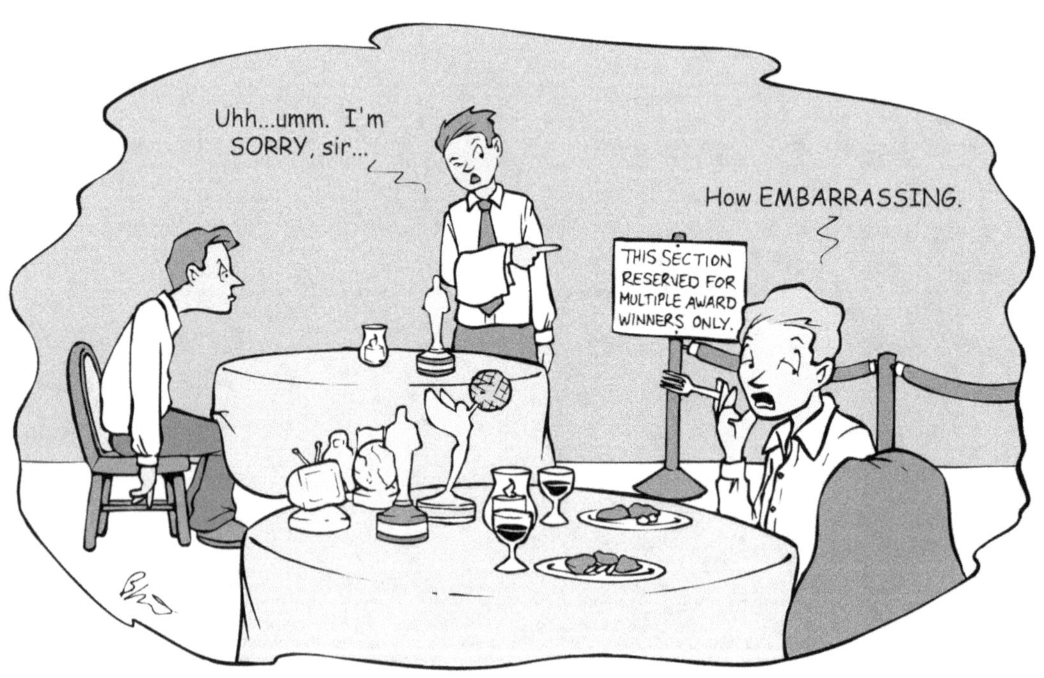

Uhh...umm. I'm SORRY, sir...
How EMBARRASSING.
THIS SECTION RESERVED FOR MULTIPLE AWARD WINNERS ONLY.

The Big "H"

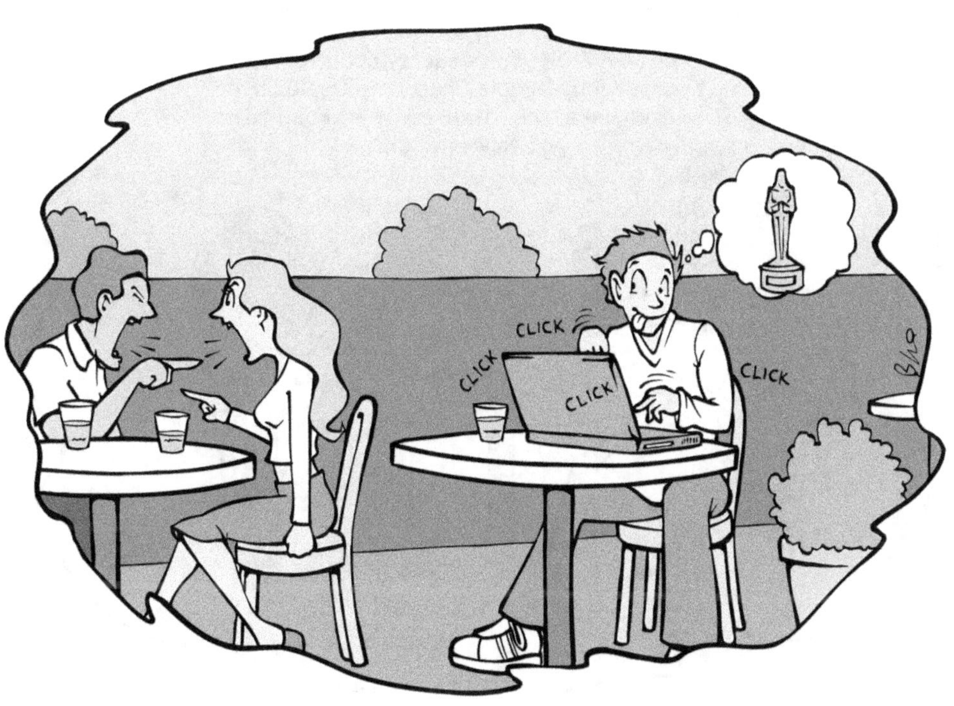

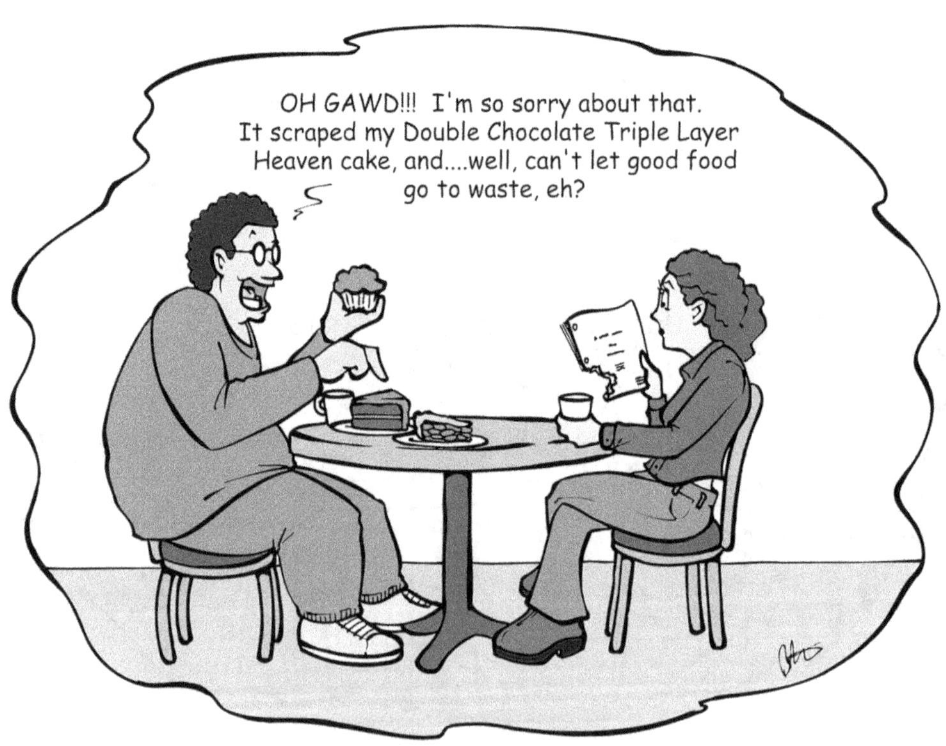

REWRITE DELAY TACTIC

The Big "H"

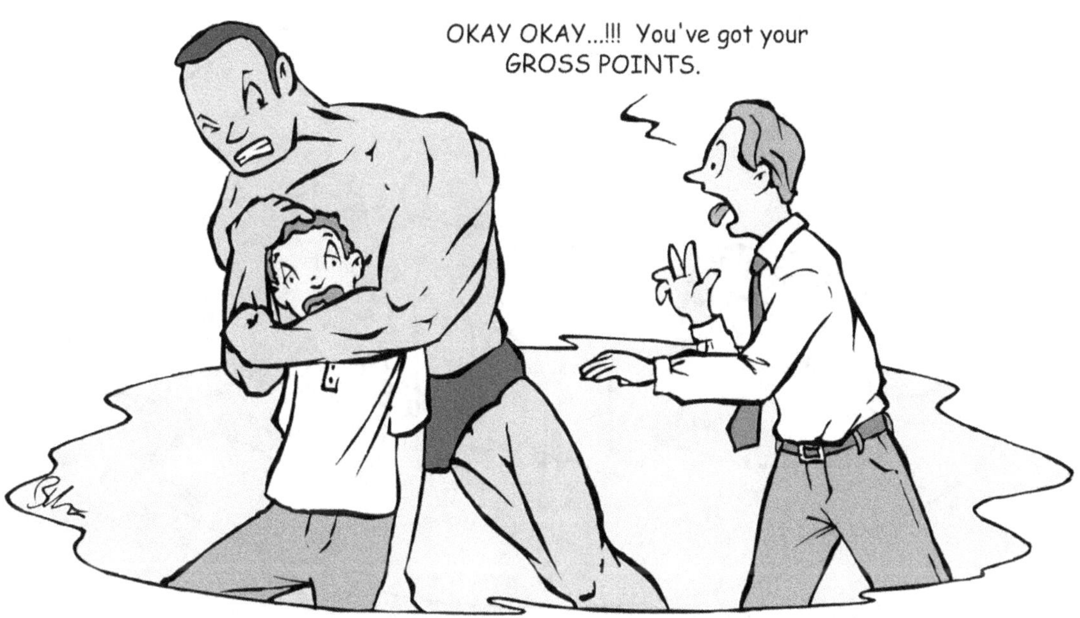

FEATURE FILM NEGOTIATING -- WWE STYLE...

The Big "H"

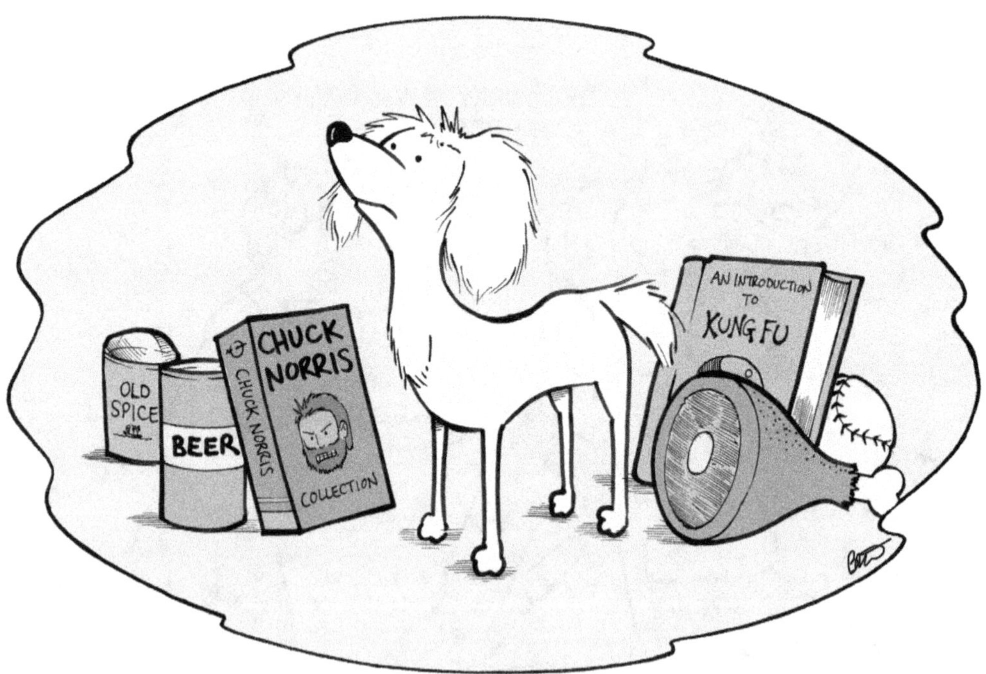

After years of life with her now-imprisoned actress owner, it became painfully clear to Precious that her new arrangements would not include a Louis Vuitton designer pet pouch.

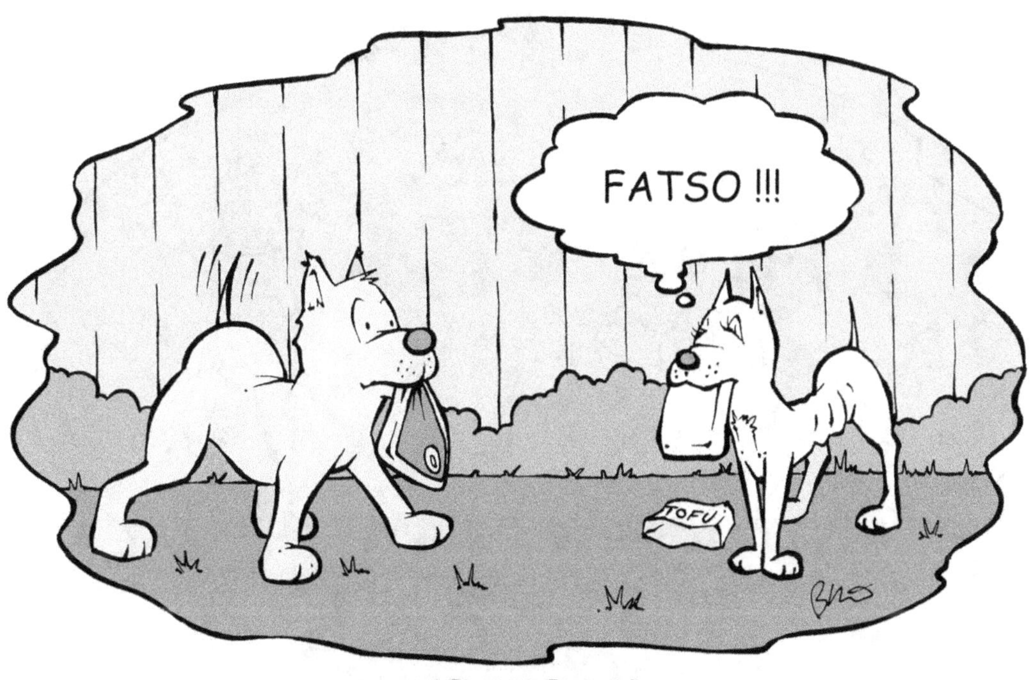

SUPERMODEL DOG

The Big "H"

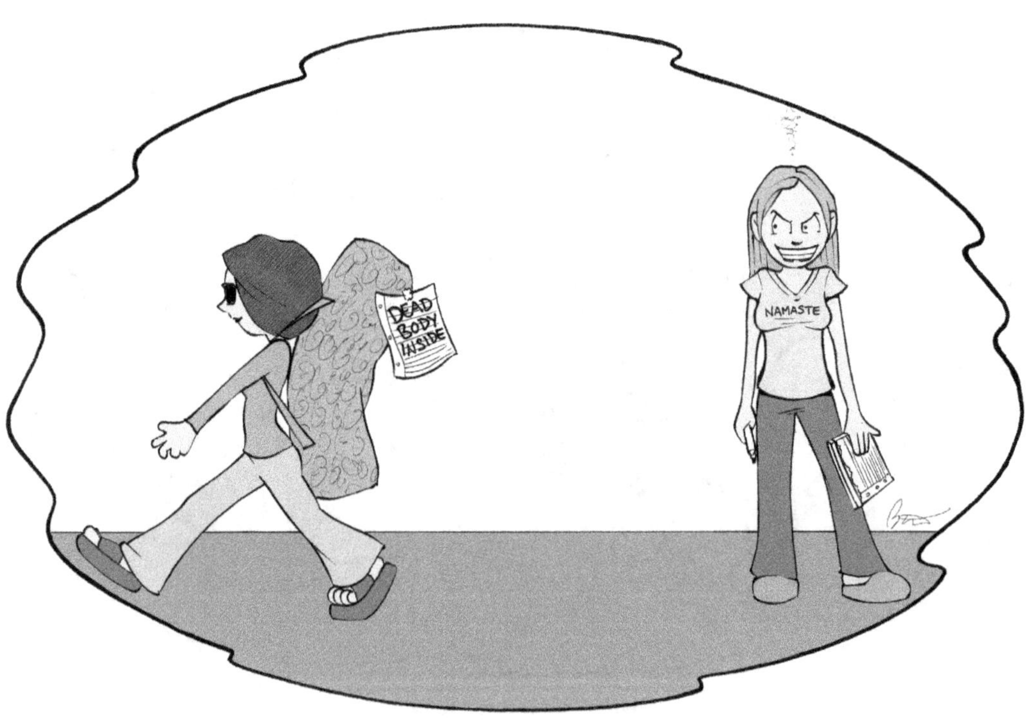

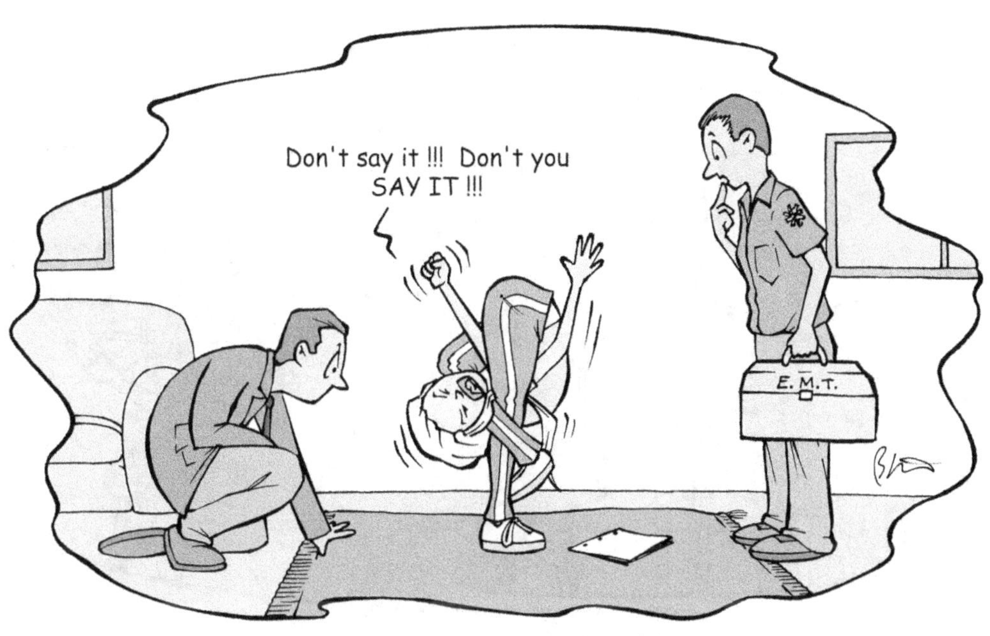

NO YOGA BEFORE A SCENE

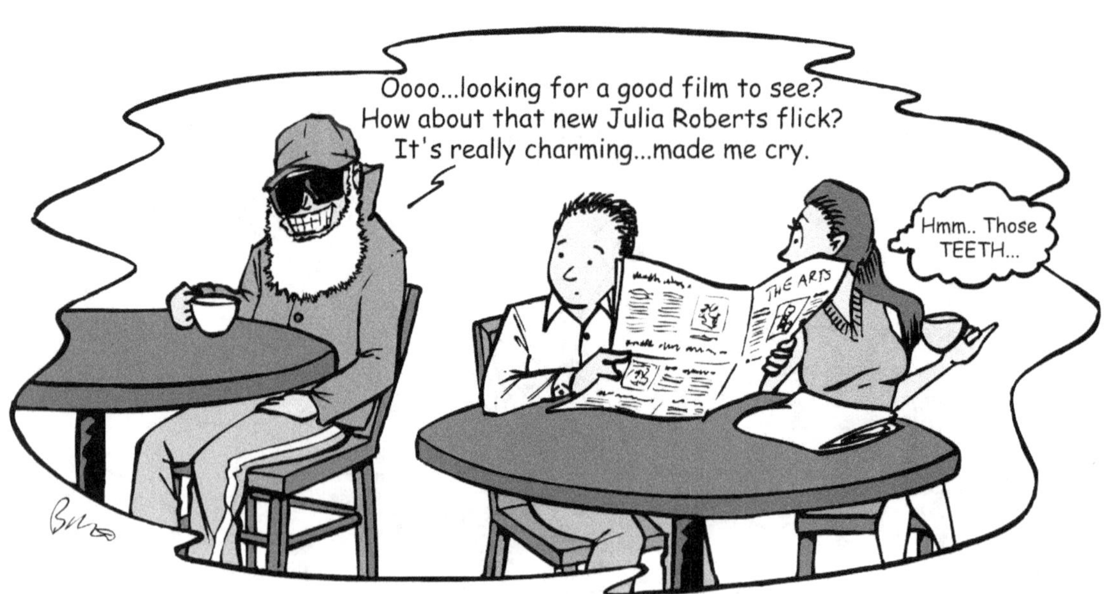

"DIRECT MARKETING" --HOLLYWOOD STYLE

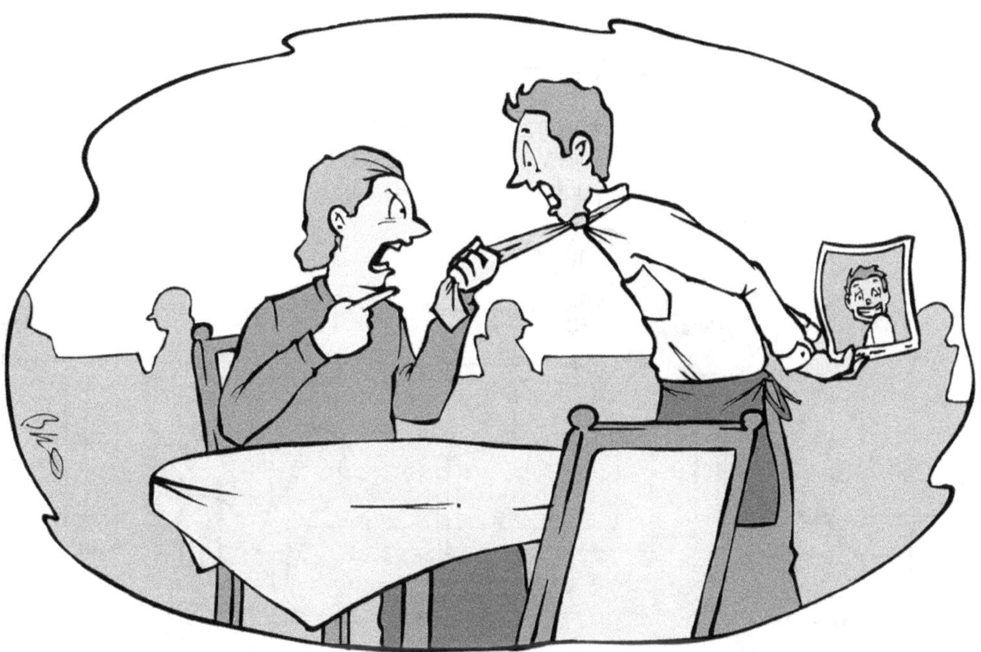

Listen, pal. I've had to deal with a valet "writer", a door man "director", and a maitre'd "producer"....so there had BETTER be a menu back there!!!

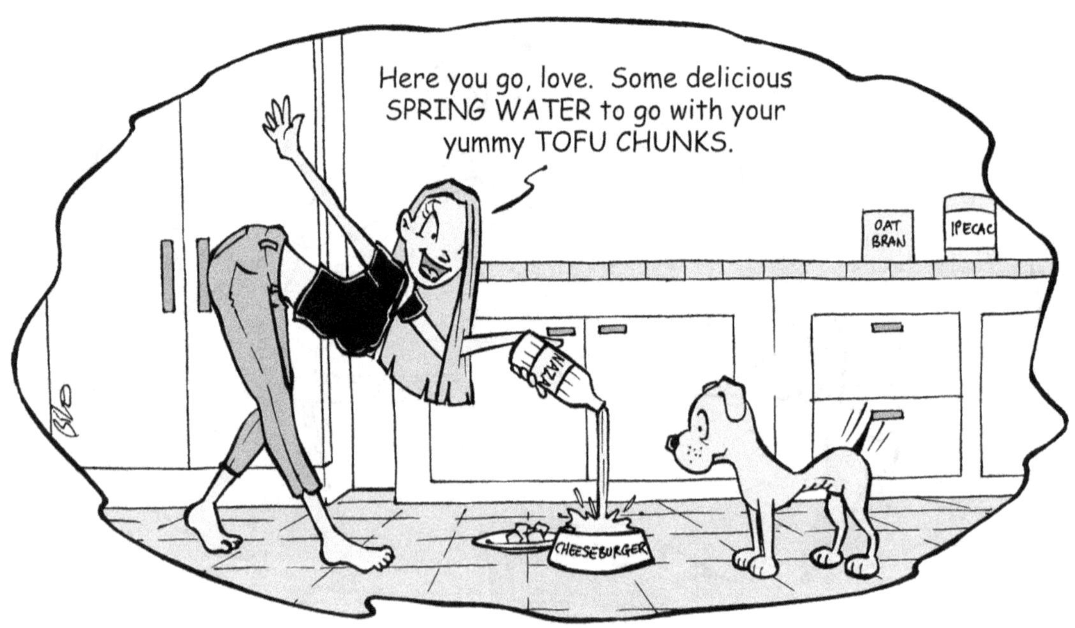

SUPERMODEL PET

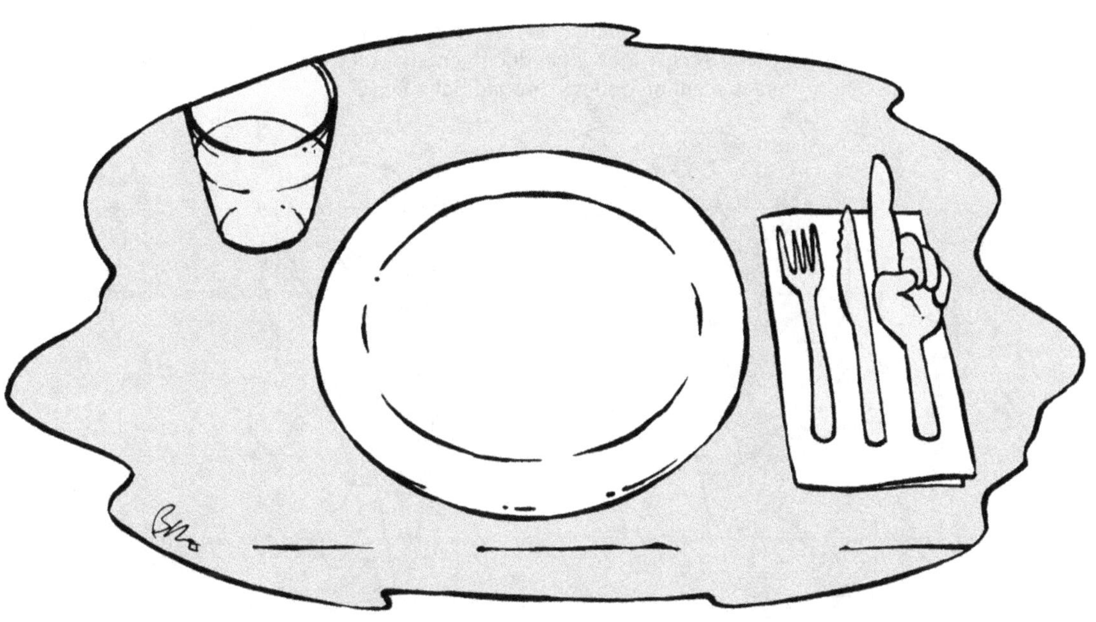

SUPERMODEL PLACE SETTING

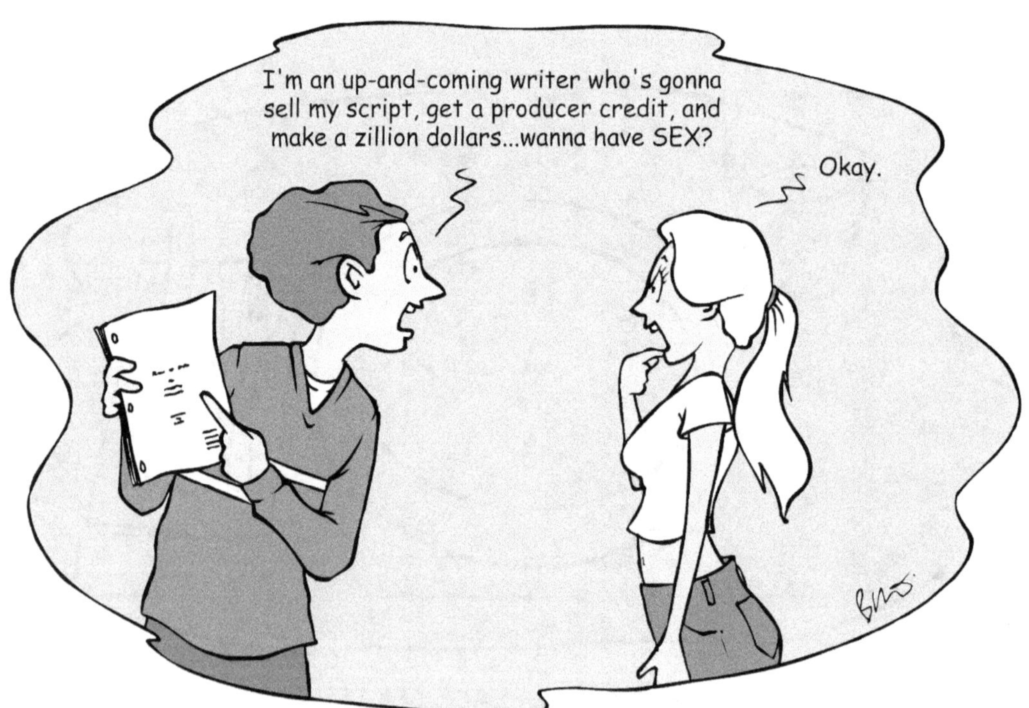

HOW UGLY WRITERS GET HOT CHICKS.

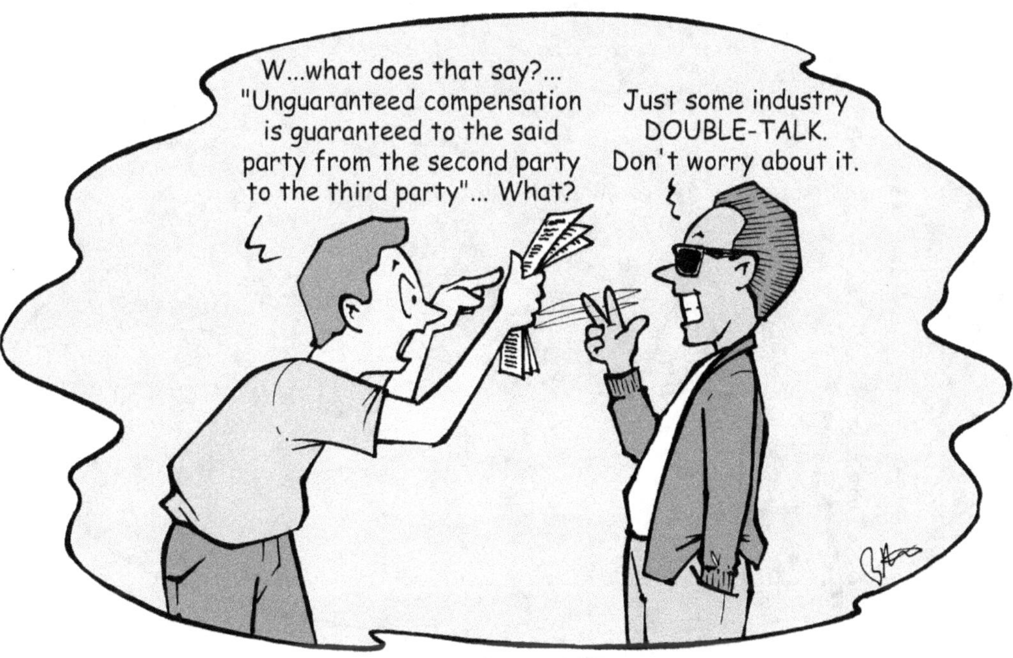

LIFE WITHOUT AGENTS

The Big "H"

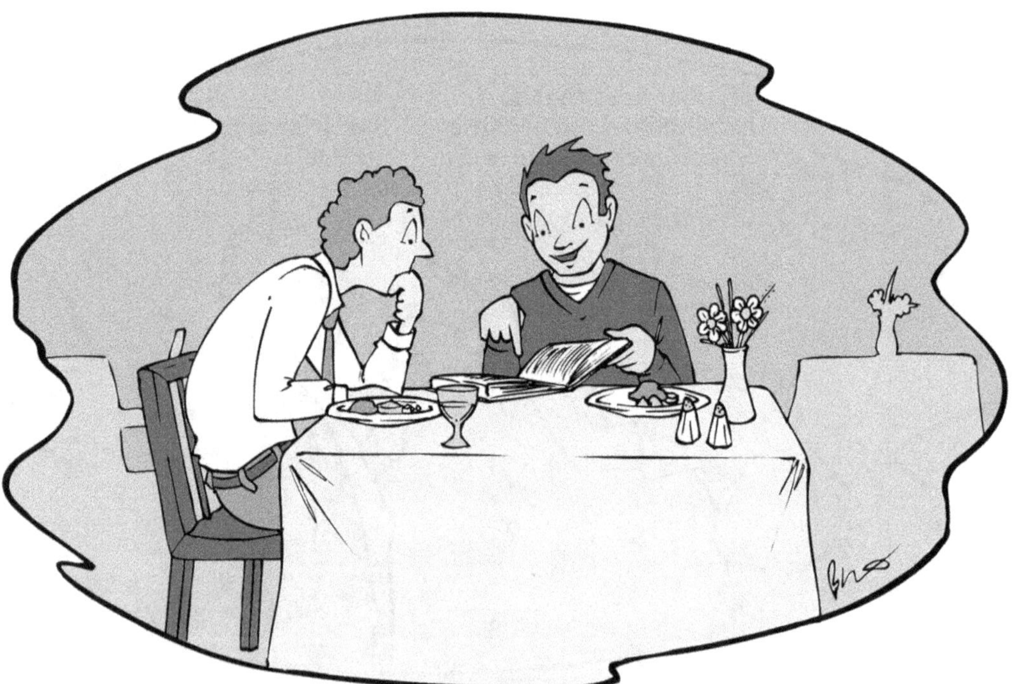

Ahhh, Pulitzer Smulitzer!! It's easy. Look, in the novel our heroine is a poor Latina domestic servant living in San Salvador. All we do is make her "white" and living in San "Fransisco" and BAM!!... instant teeny bopper coming-of-age flick.

The Big "H"

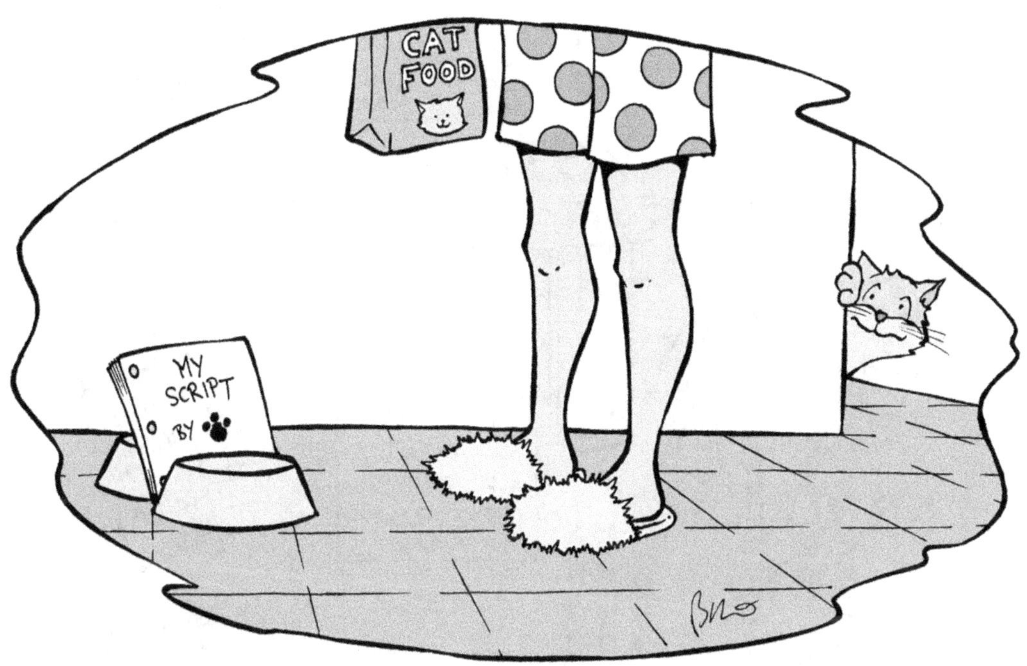

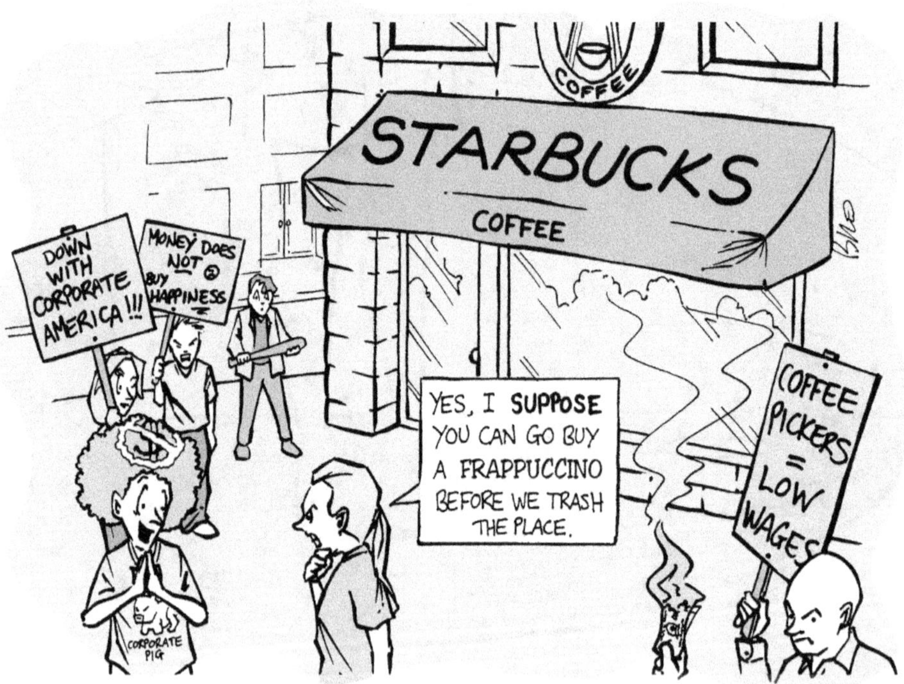
COFFEE
STARBUCKS
COFFEE
DOWN WITH CORPORATE AMERICA!!!
MONEY DOES NOT BUY HAPPINESS
YES, I SUPPOSE YOU CAN GO BUY A FRAPPUCCINO BEFORE WE TRASH THE PLACE.
COFFEE PICKERS = LOW WAGES
CORPORATE PIG

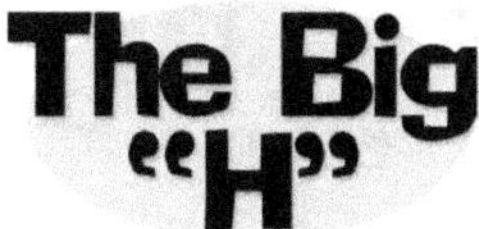

Hey!! Those muffins look great....how much? $150? Man, those must be them "French" muffins I keep hearing about. I'll take two. Man. I'm EXCITED!!!!!

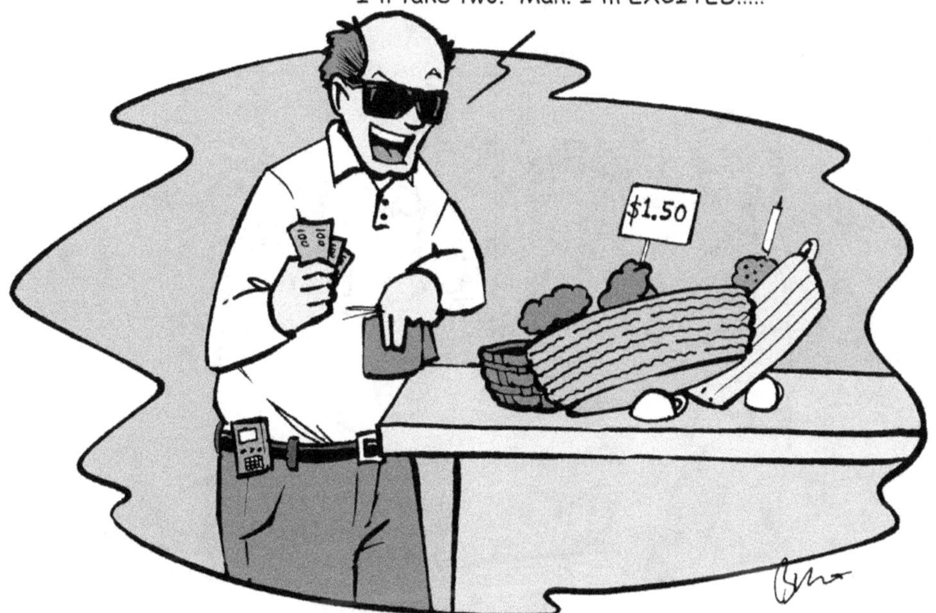

PITFALLS OF WEARING SUNGLASSES INDOORS

The Big "H"

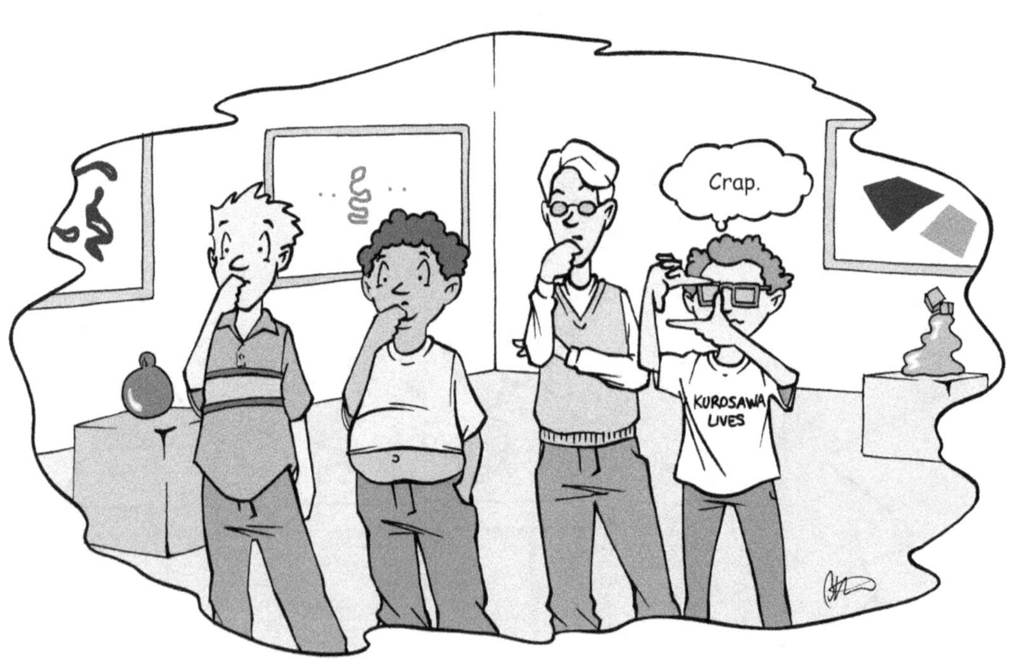

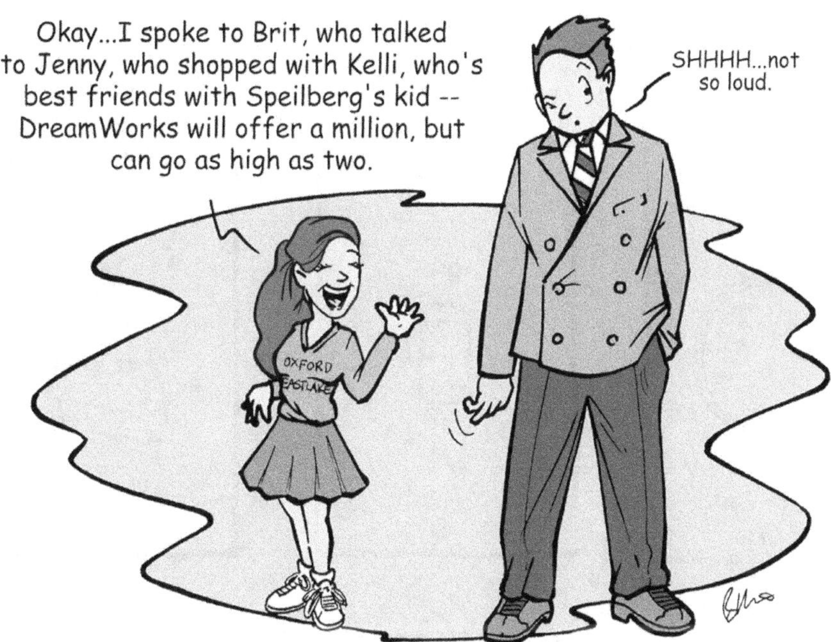

TALENT AGENT "SECRET WEAPON"

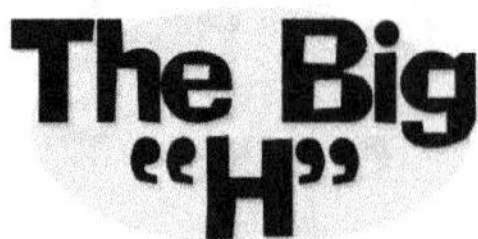

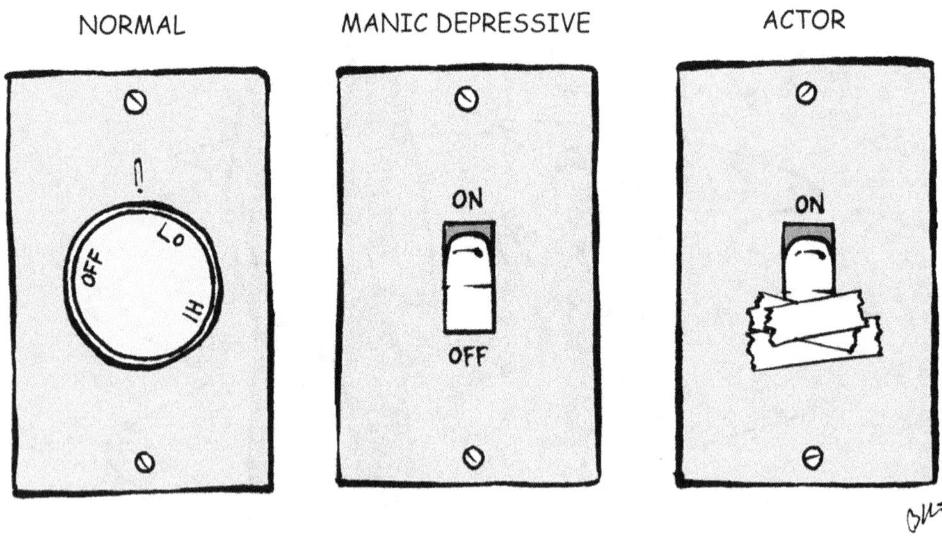

IF PEOPLE WERE LIGHT SWITCHES...

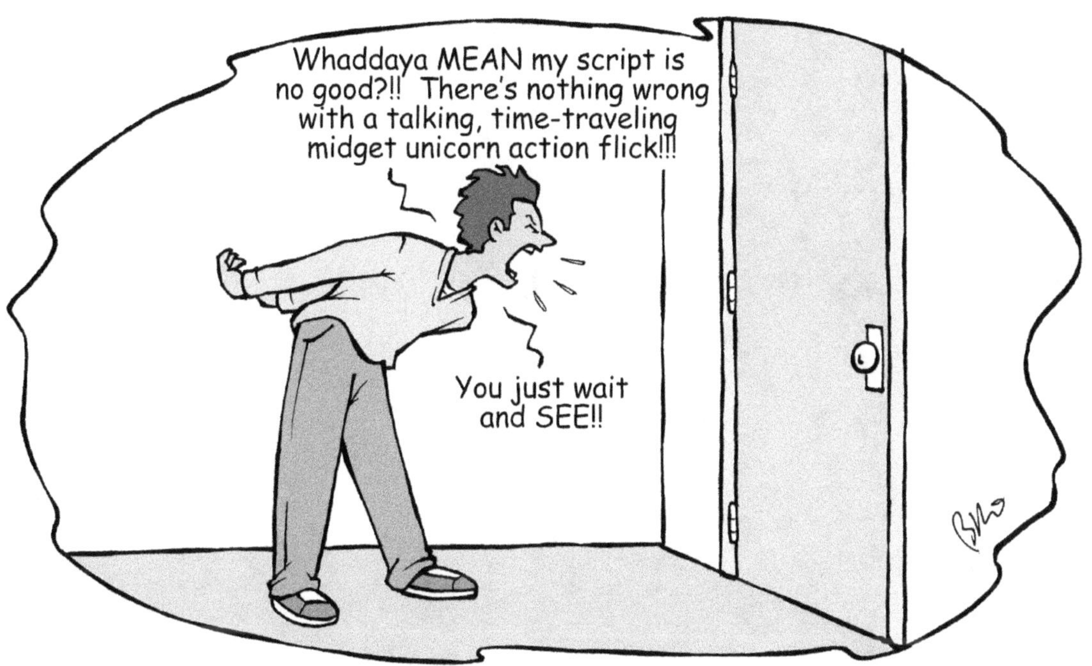

THE GREAT AMERICAN SCREENPLAY FAILS AGAIN

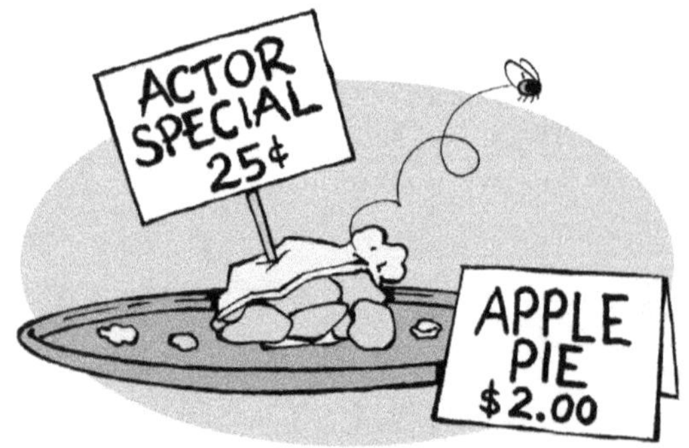

No Mas.
No Mas.

About the Fella who Draws this Stuff...

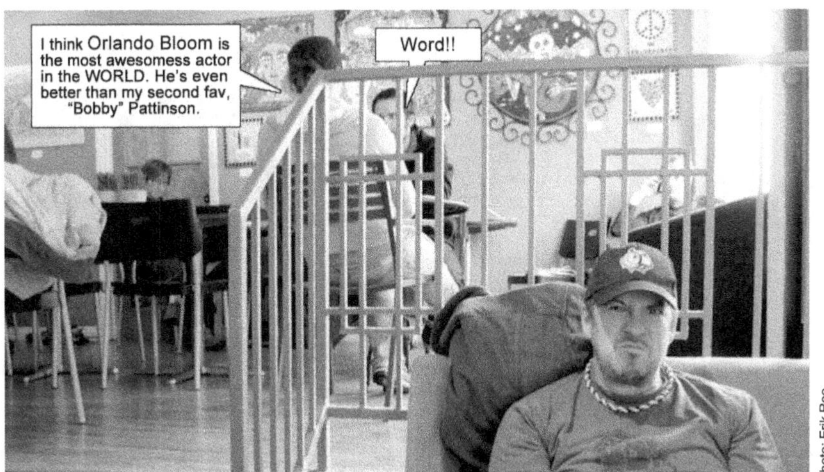

Photo: Erik Reo

Brandon Morino is an illustrator and cartoonist living in the beautiful San Fernando Valley. Surrounded by Hollywood types his entire life, the concept of creating a book of cartoons based solely upon this industry should have come naturally to him... a long **frickin'** time ago (I'm writing this in the 3rd person, so that's me being mad at myself). Alas, time heals all stupidity (at least in this case). *The Big H* is his first published cartoon compilation in the form of a book.

Brandon has supplied cartoons and humorous illustrations to publications ranging from *The Hollywood Reporter* to the *Los Angeles Daily News,* as well as children's books (*Skye the Troll*) and dozens of conceptual renderings for major PR firms, advertising houses and (yes) film productions through his company, BeelineMedia.

Brandon has many many friends who are working/non-working/working-again actors, writers, directors, singers, costume designers, and general do-anythingers. None of them were harmed in the making of this book... though I can't say the same for **THEM** harming **ME** after reading this thing.

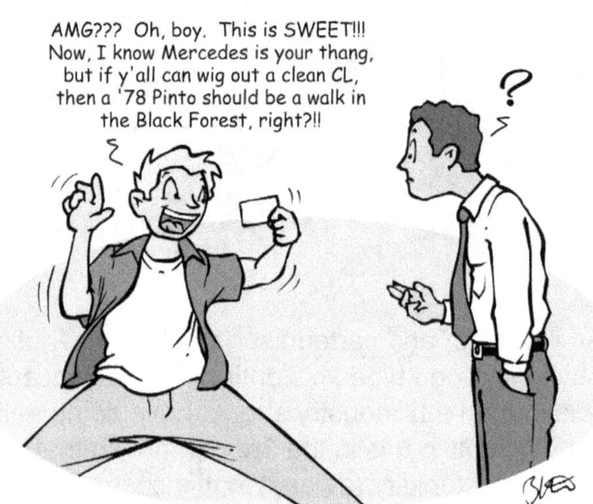

Acronyn-Deficient Newbie (ADN)

www.ingramcontent.com/pod-product-compliance
Lightning Source LLC
LaVergne TN
LVHW061225100826
845148LV00004B/861

* 9 7 8 0 6 1 5 5 6 4 6 8 5 *